PAGE after *PAGE*

Discover the confidence & passion
you need to start writing & keep writing

(no matter what!)

PAGE after PAGE

Discover the confidence & passion you need to start writing & keep writing

(no matter what!)

WRITER'S DIGEST BOOKS
CINCINNATI, OHIO
www.writersdigest.com

Heather Sellers

Visit our Web site at www.writersdigest.com for information on more resources for writers. To receive a free weekly e-mail newsletter delivering tips and updates about writing and about Writer's Digest products, register directly at our Web site at http://newsletters.fwpublications.com.

13 12 11 10 09   5 4 3 2 1

Library of Congress Has Catalogued Hardcover Edition As Follows:

Sellers, Heather
  Page after page: discover the confidence & passion you need
  to start writing & keep writing (no matter what!) / by Heather
  Sellers.
    p. cm.
  ISBN 1-58297-312-1 (alk. paper)
    I. Authorship. 1. Title.
PN147.S38 2004   2004053030
808'.02—dc22   CIP
ISBN-10: 1-58297-618-X (pbk.; alk. paper)
ISBN-13: 978-1-58297-618-1 (pbk.; alk. paper)

Edited by Kelly Nickell
Designed by Lisa Buchanan
Illustrations by Paine Proffitt
Author photo by Steven DeJong
Production coordinated by Robin Richie

Also by Heather Sellers

Spike and Cubby's Ice Cream Island Adventure
Drinking Girls and Their Dresses
Georgia Under Water

About the Author

Heather Sellers was born in Orlando and
grew up in Florida. She is an associate professor of English with a Ph.D. in writing.
She teaches fiction, poetry, nonfiction, and
community writing workshops. She has won
an NEA fellowship, and her book of stories,
Georgia Under Water, was a selection of the
Barnes & Noble New Discover program. She
lives in Holland, Michigan.

Dedication

This book is dedicated to Canton Women's Running: Nancy Auster, Debi Backus, Alex Bolis, Teresa Brownell, Carol Coakley, Kathy Duffany, Bonnie Hays-Erlichman, Betsy Kepes, Julie Kremer, Linda Potter, Carol Pynchon, and Marianne Wennrich.

Acknowledgments

Grateful acknowledgment to Al Viebranz, the Kohlberg Foundation, and St. Lawrence University for generous support and a beautiful home, 21 Elm Street. For support during the school year, thank you to Charlotte Ward and Kate ten Haken; gratitude to Hope College for summer support. Thanks to Emma Turrell for the daily art offerings.

I want to thank my teachers: Lynda Barry, Martha Beck, the late Jerome Stern, and, always, Janet Burroway.

Ann Turkle, Dick Holm, Linda Potter, Therese Stanton, Natalia Singer, Dana Lamers, Laura Woltag, and Lomeda Montgomery read early drafts of this project and their responses were invaluable.

I am most deeply indebted to my editor, Kelly Nickell.

Table of Contents

PART 1
BLANK PAGES: CREATING A NEW WRITING SELF

Look closely at the state of mind you create when you begin
something new.

Balance the necessary isolation writing requires with books,
writers, and classes.

Are you being realistic about the attention you give to
your writing time? Are you not writing because you are
unconsciously generating self-defeating messages?

Now that you have worked on your mind-set, what is it you
need to begin a passionate, confident writing life, one that
will really work?

Some writers love them. Others don't. How you can use this time-tested tool to increase your writing power.

The pure pleasure of words! How successful writers incorporate reading into their writing lives.

The one technique you must develop in order to truly become a writer.

Does everyone want to be a writer? It takes an enormous amount of time and work. How to tell if you really want to write, or if that impulse is actually part of something else.

Your parents, believe it or not, are probably co-authoring your writing life. How to use your knowledge of where you come from to develop more confidence in yourself as a writer.

The single most common reason writers do not write. How to manage anxiety is essential to finding the pleasure in your writing practice.

What happens when you don't write every day? Can breaks from writing ever be useful? Why is it so hard to start (again)?

Learning how to learn (as a writer) is key to your success in this new endeavor. A fresh look at how you grow as a writer, with tips on how to stay fluid, vibrant, and open to new knowledge.

PART 2
TURNING PAGES: HOW TO MAINTAIN YOUR COMMITMENT TO WRITING

What do you do when you don't feel like writing? How to handle the inevitable "don't-want-to-write" mood.

How do you get better as a writer? Doggedly embracing your bad writing as well as your good. Tenacity is more crucial to success than talent!

Not sure what to write about? A guaranteed method for staying in touch with the material that will lead to successful writing.

A technique for distracting your mind, letting time slip away, and getting your writing done.

Claiming the title "writer" for yourself can be thrilling, terrifying, or out of the question entirely. Why is the word *writer* so ... loaded? Will saying it hex you? Will not saying it block you?

PART 3
NEW PAGES: FINDING YOUR PLACE IN THE WORLD OF WRITING

After writing success, what happens to your writing life?

Learn how to befriend the writers you will meet.

Rejection is part of the writer's life and there's no escaping it. Discover how to gracefully reject rejection (and have a little fun doing it).

Celebrate your writing successes in an honest, authentic, and productive way.

Introduction

HOW TO STAY LIMBER, HOW TO MAKE THE WRITING NOT grim, how to enjoy writing. How to make room in *real life* for a writing life. These are my goals. Are they yours, too?

I want my readers to be able to set up a positive, happy, easy writing life. One that is fun. I believe you can (and fairly quickly) create a writing life where the writing process itself is so enchanting and delicious, you want to write. You go to the desk willingly, stress*less*ly. In my dream vision for your writing life, you don't have to make yourself write. It's not work. It's not tedious or punishing. It's what you do. A happy, productive writing life is like a simple, perfect dinner, or prayer and meditation. It's soul food.

So many of my students practice a weird, contorted relationship to writing. In fact, many of the (struggling) writers I know have adopted or internalized a bunch of rules that they then proceed to break every single day. They set up regimens, word counts, page goals. They nurture secret fantasies of prizes and publications. Then, they say they aren't disciplined. They say they are lazy. They say they have a terrible procrastination problem. They claim they want to write, and they act as though they can't understand why they don't write. Ultimately, they don't write very much, but they wish to, very badly.

I'm surrounded by nonwriter want-to-be-writers. Probably you are too. I see so many of my students, friends, and colleagues pushing themselves lower, lower, lower. I saw my mom do it. My dad does it. My students do it. So many of us use writing as a way to keep ourselves down, limited, stuck.

This book teaches the person who wants to write how to simplify and clarify the habits and states of mind conducive to writing. It's easy to use mystery as an excuse. It's tempting to say we don't understand the muse, the artistic process, greatness. But really, we do. My hope is that I can present, in practical chapters, a course of lessons that will help stuck, nervous, scared, lazy writers (is that not all of us?) break through to their best material, and welcome into their lives a writing practice that feeds rather than sucks and demands.

Almost anyone can write good stuff.

It's a matter of sitting down, conjuring a state of complete dedication and complete openness, and writing. Putting pen to page.

Okay. So, I know. This writing business—it's really, really hard to do. Like anything that looks effortless and beautiful—cliff-diving, racing, dancing—writing takes an almost inhuman ability to focus. Creating a writing life requires growth and self-knowledge on your part. There will be bumps in the road as you become a writer: parts that are boring, lonely, tedious, silly, selfish, and extremely frustrating. That's all a part of writing. And in truth, writing is the most difficult thing I do in a day.

But it's not the writing part that's so hard. Good writing *will* flow out of you, easily. It's the setup, the preparation, the habits of mind, the thoughts you think before and during your writing—that's what is so hard to get right. Preparing is complex. Writing is simple.

My method asks you to look gently at what you love. If you love writing, it helps you stay in a good mood, a happy mood. Writing helps you know who you are, and how you think, and what you need. For many of us, it's not just a way to express, impress, or vent, it's a whole spiritual practice. The stuff you have to do to get good at writing is the exact same stuff you have to do when you want a relationship—with a lover, a parent, a child—to go well. It's how you become a better, healthier, more balanced person—it's all the same work, this work we have to do to become "real" writers.

The life part is hard.

The writing part does not have to be hard.

Clearing out bad habits and weird mind-sets can take a lot of bold confidence. What will come out once you are *ready* to write, once you are prepared to see writing as a way and not an end to something? I don't know. That's between you, the muse, and your compost pile of fabulous material.

What I can teach you is how to set up your life in a clear way so you can actually get some writing done. I want to help you keep the pleasure in writing. I want to help you avoid the dull mind games that come with trying to make a writing life.

So, here's my proposal: Invite yourself into the writing life like you invite a lover upstairs. Want to see my best stuff? Want to play, all night, want me to lavish myself on you?

That is the right attitude toward your new writing life. Seductive, pleasure-seeking, and fun.

Now, you might be a shy lover. You might not wear satin, red slinky things. Or, you might be a monogamous, in-the-dark-only quiet kind of person. You might be wild on the page, and quite conservative in your daily life.

You might be bold in bed, and feel like you are really good, and why has no one discovered this and married/published you?

Well.

Good writers are writers with a few tricks up their sleeves. I want to show you how to develop and sharpen your own tricks—tricks for staying in your writing chair, and for getting there in the first place.

In *Writing Down the Bones*, Natalie Goldberg says that "to do writing practice means to deal ultimately with your whole life." In *Page After Page*, by showing how I have navigated, for better and for worse, the challenges of writing, working, teaching, publishing, loving, friending, owning a dog, doing laundry, I hope to inspire you to first get past your initial, perfectly normal counterproductive resistance, and on to words, your words, on the pages.

Your words, your pages.

The lessons here are the ones I learn again and again. This book is also a kind of autobiography of my last fifteen years writing and teaching and publishing. An alternative title could be *Girl Poet Takes on the University Life!* It's in part my coming-of-age memoir, a book about how I learned to learn. It's also a window into my classroom, where I hope you, alongside my students, will learn how to take useful lessons from any class, any teacher.

The chapters in this book explain how I found out what kind of writing life was right for me, and what kinds of exercises and books I found useful along the way. This book is, I hope, like sitting down with me, in my living room, over tea. I'll tell you my story and ask you for yours, dragging books and writing down off the shelves. You might be looking over my shoulder at the wonderful art on my walls. I'll say this: Try to get past your taste. Try to learn from *everything*.

Every writer is a little different. But all people who write have similar fears and blocks about writing. Most of my writing students fall into predictable pits and traps. I want to tell you what I know about the writing path, and, I hope, give you some equipment so you can build bridges over the traps. There are fabulous treasures and wondrous rewards and great wise people along the way.

How do we begin?

By writing!

Part 1

Blank Pages: Creating a New Writing Self

Chapter 1

The First Day

THE FIRST DAY OF ANYTHING IS STRANGE AND WONDERFUL and exciting. You want to write. You sit down with a new book (like this one!) on the writing life. You think, *This will be good.*

But starting something new is often difficult and annoying. It's never exactly what you expected.

Yet another book on how to write. You don't really like these books. Or, the book is okay, but you still aren't *writing.* You take a writing class. Your fellow students are not great writers. They are perhaps irritating, pompous, or speaking in clichés. The teacher is a little … weird.

My first day in a new yoga class is always all about trying to like the teacher—*he is not like my old teacher.* He is the new teacher. He seems a little sweaty, a little large. I always think: *I am not going to like this. He will never understand.* I am always nervous on the first day, and my nervousness takes the form of *disliking the teacher.*

I have taught many writing workshops, and on the first day there is always this funny dynamic. A kind of love/hate, push-me/pull-you energy.

Recently I taught a group of retired women, women who wanted to start writing. On the first Saturday morning, we all gathered in the little basement room where class would meet each week.

We introduced ourselves, and then I said in my perky friendly way, "Okay, let's warm up. We're going to write *a lot* today. And don't worry if your writing is terrible."

"This is not a good exercise," the tall, beautiful woman in the front row said a few minutes into our writing. "I don't understand what you want."

Her friend repeated this. "I don't understand what you want from us!"

The beautiful tall woman pulled at the collar of her crisp white blouse and smoothed her hair. She was frustrated, and she wasn't writing. She put her pencil in her perfectly lipsticked red mouth. She, and all the women, glared at me.

I smiled at the women and nodded. *This is resistance,* I thought. This was me just last Monday night in yoga class. I continued with the writing practice I wanted my students to do. "Try to listen to your thoughts, instead of thinking, instead of driving them. Try to let them come up, from deep inside you. Write those down. Writing is more of a *listening* activity than a performing action."

A few minutes later, I noticed in the back row a very quiet woman, reading through my handouts. She wasn't writing, either. She looked up, a kind of scared rabbit look in her soft brown eyes. She said softly, "This class is going to be really time-consuming. I don't think it's realistic. Not realistic at all! We have lives!"

"Really!" said the two friends.

"This is just not what I expected," a yellow sweat suit-wearing woman chimed in. "Not at all what I thought it'd be like."

All my students want to want to learn to write. Just like when we go to any workshop or class, or even on a date. We want to write, we really, really do. We have fabulous intentions. We prepare, with notebooks, pens, books on writing (or cologne, a new outfit). We walk into new situations, new endeavors, ready and willing. New writing books, Web sites, teachers, ideas—yes!

And we often run out, screaming our heads off. *That was terrible! That was not what I wanted.*

Isn't it funny how quickly our resistance rises?

In our minds, it is so easy to say yes—*yes,* I will meditate; *yes,* I will be calm and not yell at my family members/roommates; *yes,* I will walk thirty minutes every day; *yes,* I will eat more fiber; *yes,* I will write, I will write, I will write. In our minds we say: I'll incorporate more writing, better writing, into my life.

Then, when it comes down to doing the new thing, we say *no.*

In so many ways, big and small, we say no. Can't do it.

The thing we want seems good in our head; the reality of practicing it feels very different. We tend to sketch out how things *should be* and then they play out quite differently. We don't like that.

I want to learn to write (date better caliber people/do yoga/swim/stop smoking/play squash/stop being so busy).

But not this way.

I want to learn the new thing. Not in *this* way.

That's how it was, exactly, for me. I wanted to learn some more yoga techniques. I signed up for class and paid in advance. I bought a new sticky mat, and another book on yoga. I went to my first class. I sat cross-legged. I wanted to learn yoga. But not from that teacher who was chubby and odd and not really very good.

I ended up dropping out of yoga after three sessions. And, I wish someone would have told me a long time ago: Whenever you take a class or buy a book or start a new endeavor, it won't be how you expect. You have to figure out how to learn from that class. That book. That particular endeavor. You have to let it teach you.

Resistance is our way of shutting down fear. Fear is unpleasant. We avoid it—that makes sense. It is delicious to blame the chubby, sweaty, not-great yoga teacher. To insist we need Better Instruction. That sounds really, really convincing and good.

But what happens is not good: I didn't do any yoga. I'm still not better at yoga. I took a Pilates class, and I didn't like that teacher either!

Resistance is a powerful, pervasive, energy-blocking force. To weaken it, simply shine a little light in there.

On the first day you take on anything new, here is what you can expect—plan for it:

1. You will not like the tone/hair color/smell/shape/quality of the instruction. You will feel you are wasting your money and your time. This is your desperate attempt to get out of change, which is very threatening to the Self. Here's what you do. Say: Thank you for your concerns, but I'm going to go ahead and do my best work, in spite of the limitations of my new chosen direction.

2. You will doubt you are as good as the other people in the class/reading the book/sticking their butts up into

the air. You will simultaneously feel you are significantly better than the other people. This is your ego. Shine light on it, which will quiet it down, and say: Comparing myself to others doesn't help me learn anything. I'm going to do my best work, and focus solely on my own self for the next twenty minutes, but thanks for the input!

3. You will have great intentions, and truly, when you buy this new writing book (exer-ball, ab-ercizer, diet journal, free weights, self-improvement tapes) you do imagine a whole new way of life, with you diligently working a new program. Intentions are good, but let's not focus on them, because their evil twin is resistance. You will probably have a push-me/pull-you relationship with your early writing practice. Successful writers anticipate this. They cultivate the ability to be aware of the mind without being sucked into their mind.

On the first day of your new writing practice, you will feel exhilarated, inept, argumentative, self-indulgent, bold, silly, inferior, brilliant, blessed, and confused. That's a lot of emotion to stir up. Plan on it—and set yourself up for a good first day by saying this: Twenty minutes of writing.

No more. No less.

Try not to think very much.

Acknowledge the busy beehive of thoughts and fears quickly, and dismiss as much as you can. Thanks for the input, Self, but I have this project, and I am going to go ahead and do this. I'll let you know if I need any more inner guidance. Right now, I think I'm fine!

The trick is: Don't think. Don't think much at all. Acknowledge the thinking machine, and move on quickly.

That's the great talent of the First Day.

ON YOUR PAGE: *Exercise 1*

This is the first day of your new writing life. You need paper. It doesn't matter what paper. You need a pen. This, and a willingness to be patient with your resistance and to learn about your own funny self, is all you need.

Pen, paper, desire.

Buy notebook paper, or use white paper, or use the back of the envelopes sitting in your desk drawer. Buy a leather journal from Italy, or a watercolor sketch pad—it doesn't matter. But be careful: The purchasing of office supplies is like saying *think*. You do not want to think.

You just need paper.

Please simplify this task. Make two lists: The qualities of your ideal writing guidebook. What is covered? The qualities of your ideal writing class. What do you learn?

Make your lists as long as you can, leaving room to add new things as they come to you.

Then, make a third list. You, as a writing student, a small new pupil. What are all your best student-like qualities? Who are you when you are learning—truly open, changing, growing? Make a long list of the attitudes you have when you are loving the act of learning something. What do you look like then? What are you wearing? What do you have in the palm of your hand?

If you are having trouble, or feel tempted to do this exercise in your head, keep in mind the following:

1. *Your mind will try to keep you from writing; you can easily outsmart it by keeping it busy with information-gathering tasks.*

2. *You already know, intuitively, everything you need to know about writing well, and writing regularly. The teacher you seek is within you! I know that sounds so new-age and zazen dumb, but it is true, and I will show you your way to this teacher. It's all you have, and all you need.*

3. *Excellent writers are very articulate about how they work and why. Your first day is rightly devoted to making space in your brain, your soul, and your life for this new endeavor.*

Like yoga, or dance, or cliff-diving, starting a writing life looks, to the outside world, to the nonwriter, like nothing, so easy.

A man sits down at a desk, and writes some junk down on some scrap paper. How hard can it be?

It's really hard.

Maybe the hardest thing you have done so far.

Chapter 2
Writing You Don't Do Alone

WHEN I STARTED WRITING, IT WAS SECRET.

Writing and me, against the world. I hunkered down. I gritted my teeth because I was going to be a Writer.

All by myself, thank you very much. I didn't want to tell anyone.

To become a Writer meant you thought you were hot stuff, very bright—a brilliant and charming sort of person, a know-it-all, a snob. Not one person in my family was this kind of person. These types were mocked. "She'll have the carpet pulled out from under *her* fancy feet," my mother would say of someone who put on airs. "Hard work!" my father would refrain. "Hard work, it takes hard work." He also said, "Writing is thinking."

In truth, everyone in my family was a secret writer. No one thought it was very polite to go around discussing writing, the writing life, or one's own writing desire. It would be like talking about money or sex. Writing-desire was rudely lofty.

Writing was secret.

The only other thing that secret was masturbation, pornography, and my mother's lingerie drawer.

I only knew secrets had shame, I didn't really get that they had power, too.

When I was eighteen, I built a miniroom out of cardboard boxes in the living room of my boyfriend's house. In this house, high on a hill in Tallahassee, Florida, you could see light through the floorboards. It was a shotgun house; you came in through the front door, and walked through the living room, past my box house, into the bedroom, into the kitchen, and right out the back door. There were a lot of spiders. We had puppies instead of babies, and the box house was my place within a place. I put down a beautiful rug. I had a little green banker's lamp and my typewriter, on box tables. I had a little box blockade/door, and when I was in my writing space, no one—not the boyfriend, or the puppies, or the visitors, of which there were very few—was allowed to enter.

I thought: *To write, you have to be alone.* I knew: *To write, you have to do it in secret. Don't let anyone see you writing. Don't tell anyone about it.*

When I was twenty-one, the boyfriend and I enrolled in the local graduate program in writing. It was not a posh program; it was easy to gain admittance. Still, I was thrilled. And I was terrified I would be discovered. Which was likely, now that I had enrolled in *a writing program.*

I wrote all the time.

I spent my evenings in wild workshops talking about books and stories and poems by people who were sometimes great and often terrible writers, who, by the end of the semester, by some kind of weird group alchemy, improved.

We all improved.

I simply couldn't believe it. You suffered through the shame of writing all this crap, showed it to other people, read their crap, and you got better?

You kept writing a secret, you went at night to workshops, you never spoke about your writing, you didn't even talk while

[16]

it was being critiqued, you tried to pretend you were a normal person, going to work, the grocery store, football games.

And, as a writer, you got better.

It was weird.

And scary and powerful and true.

And contradictory.

A secret life, and within the center of that secret life, a very public noisy chattering group of people in on the same secret—hours spent alone, no talking, lying to friends and family about how you spend your time.

That year, I had two writers groups, one for poetry, one for fiction (I still do!). I had the boyfriend who was an amazing published writer and brilliant locally-famous cartoonist. My teachers invited all of the secret-public writing students over to their big messy book-filled teacher homes for big old parties where everyone talked about writers and books and affairs and Who Was Who.

I had allies. Even the people I didn't like, I considered writing allies—we were all in the soup together. We felt there was more than enough room for new members of the association, the secret society.

Do it, don't talk about it, you're in.

What I didn't realize at the time was that my life was crowded with words and the people who made them. I'd always believed my writing life was happening only when I was in the box house.

My writing life was, and is, everywhere, in every hour of my life.

I was a very tormented person when I was twenty-one, and I felt very isolated. I had known no other life. I felt on the fringes. I was quiet and shy and uncomfortable around people, and uncomfortable in my own skin. It felt tight on me, and itchy. I didn't realize I was surrounded by active, dreaming, writing writers. I took them all for granted.

In the next decade, I would enter into the most painful dry period—a kind of blocked period that lasted years—and I didn't notice for a long time I'd lost contact with the box house energy. I didn't *need* to carve out a space anymore. I didn't have workshops with terrible writers in them. I had graduate degrees. And a teaching job. And I had been completely and utterly outed as a writer. Everyone knew. I felt like I was standing on stage, bare naked, in the spotlight, with a microphone. With nothing to say.

But writing, writing you don't do alone.

It took me a long time to realize I was still surrounded by that secret clan of wonderful, bad, weird, and brilliant fellow writers.

When you creep into your box house at night after the parties, when you wake up early to write at your computer in a dark room with just the green-gray glow of the screen lighting your way, you are not alone.

Writing is a communal act. You have all your teachers' words funneling through you, your words, your character's words, the books on your bookshelves—it's really pretty loud, writing. Writing is a dance with all those other books you've read and the ones you're going to read. Writing is making a house within the house.

You aren't ever alone doing it.

The House of Writing is filled with a bunch of noisy mostly kind folks yakking their heads off.

What you do as you embark on a writing life, on day two of your new life, and for the whole rest of it is this: You learn to listen.

You want to surround your hours with choruses—books and writers and words of the highest quality, in as many forms as you can import into your world.

You might need to spend more time at your typewriter so you can listen to the deep, deep thing inside you. You might already be spending enough time at your keyboard—it might be the quality, shape, and content of all the other hours that need your attention right now.

What does the rest of your life look like? Are you letting the muse know you are serious about this writing business? Or are you only serious when you are in your box house? Are you saturating your life with writing-life stuff?

Practice. Surround yourself with writers. Who will they be? Surround yourself with books. What will you read? Cultivate teachers. Who is in your backyard who can teach you something about writing?

(Your first answer might be a cranky, "No one! I live in Kansas, in a cornfield! I'm young, I have no money! No car!" That would be *resistance*. It's okay to go back to chapter one.)

Writing as a way of life, writing in a way that will save your life, has a very interesting dynamic to it. To be successful as a writer, you have to cultivate two oppositional sides of your personality: the secret-keeper you, and the public chatty bold you. They're both in there, and they both deserve the honor of practice.

At times you are in your own version of the box house, writing your work. What do you want to take into that room?

Remember, you are what you eat. You are whomever you are with. Fill your plate with fabulous words and their originators.

At the same time, what do you need to keep secret? I look at it this way: You know that goofy new-age saying on t-shirts and magnets everywhere, *Dance as if no is watching*? Well, you have to write as if no one will ever know you write. Ever.

Keep your output a secret for a while. Make what comes out of you very, very private. Jane Hamilton visited my campus last week, and she said the best thing for her writing is living in a town of six hundred people where no one really asks her, and she doesn't talk about the Writing Life. Ever.

There are three essential reasons you have to shut up about your writing. If you talk about your writing life, you are siphoning off valuable needed energy that must be fed right into the page. You must convert some of that yakking into pages. Be quiet, and a tension will build up in you. Keep secrets, and they'll have no choice but to come out in another way—not the way of gossip, but the way of the page.

Second, if you talk about it, you aren't doing it.

Third, as a writing beginner, you have one main goal: to increase your confidence in yourself as a writer. You need to stop talking, which can be heard by your own baby writing self as bragging, false promises, killing expectations.

Be quiet. Conserve energy. Do not speak—to anyone right now—of your writing desires.

Silence yourself in order to speak more meaningfully, from a deeper, truer place—I promise this works.

At the same time, do the opposite. Football players balance the raw energy of strength training with ballet. Musicians practice and learn theory. Architects do math and art, bakers science and craft, chemistry and icing formed into bunnies. Most practitioners in any field use very different, even contradictory sets of muscles or skills or mind-sets.

Writers have to be very secretive. They also have to be very communal. Successful writers learn how to navigate between the two states without using lazy-mind as an excuse to not.

The yakking you is just as important as the quiet you. The trick (and this will take a lot of practice—be patient as you develop this skill) is to be able to choose and conjure the appropriate productive state, on command.

Make your input—the stuff you take in to feed your writing—very communal. Find out what everyone else knows. Immerse yourself in the rivers—books, writers, readers—that feed the ocean of writing.

Ask every writer you meet for insights into the practice of writing. Read every book like this one you can get your hands on. Watch for your resistance, and use it as a guide to see what you need to learn more about. Be sure you meet with other writers (just tell your family you are going to a meeting) who are at your same level—floundering, fearful, terrible wonderful beginners. You must take a class in writing, and then ten more. Every class won't be great, but every interaction you initiate between other writers can be. Be the nosy person who asks lots of questions—and listens carefully to the answers. Go to every live reading, every literary party at your library; go to every book-signing and open mic. Your task in all this is to learn how to be with other writers. Don't—*do not*—talk about your work. Most successful writers say, simply, "I have a new project I'm working on." That's it. Shut up. Say no more.

That's the secret part.

What to talk about with your writing community, which will be ever-growing, maybe tiny, and always changing? The good books, and why; the good teachers, and why; the good writing conferences, and why; the good classes, and why; the good bookstores, and why; who is in love with who, and why; who has great coffee, and why ... you get the idea. You can do this online, but there's nothing like being with—smelling and see-ing and breathing the same air as—other working writers.

Input equals public.

Output equals private.

ON YOUR PAGE: *Exercise 2*

Writing is both a very secret, private gesture as well as a communal activity. Whether you like it or not. You can be solitary, or you can be Mr. Popular, it doesn't really matter. The words coming in all day are the words you have to work with and you must have a sacred space in your personality that is totally silent. The flow of words that you were born to write down must have a silent chamber in you in which to reverberate. On day two of your new writing life, work on becoming more conscious of the interplay between the secret silent writing zone, and the necessity of meaningful interaction. It's like learning a new dance. Your switch back and forth will be probably clumsy at first—I hate being alone in a room! I hate talking to groups of people I don't know!—but this is the stock and trade of the writing life. This is what you will be doing when you are a writer. It's fine if you are ter-rible at these two things now—most beginners are. You just do them anyway, and no one minds that you are terrible at sitting alone and keeping secrets, and that you're really not very socially skilled—no one cares. You are a writer. This is what writers do.

In order to train yourself in the interplay between public writing self and private writing self, here are some things to do this week. And remember, to develop your public writing self (and most writers are shy, so this might be the harder of the two), be patient; these exercises might be painful. But they'll give you amazing results!

a. *Write on your scratch paper the answers to these questions: Do you want your "input" to look any different? Does your communal writing self need to be balanced, enriched? What would you need to do? What does your dream writing community look like? Who helps you with what, and what do you help others with, by way of the writing life? Write for twenty minutes.*

b. *To enrich your public writing self, join a book group, or find an online book group or at least some lists of books other writers love. Or, sub-scribe to* The New York Times Book Review *or another source. You need to be connected with other people who are involved with books— living your writing life away from books isn't an option. Spend one hour connecting with other readers. Can you commit to an hour a week of talking with others about books and their makers? Find smart, fun peo-ple by looking at libraries, colleges, newspapers, and bookstores for groups. If this is nerve-racking, break it down into very small steps and do one each day for a whole week. Call one library today and ask if there is a book group. On another day, go to your local bookstore, and buy one book review magazine. On another day, talk to one other per-son (e-mail is okay!) about a book you will both read or have read. Practice doing the kinds of things writers do when they are not writing.*

c. *Design a reading program. Create a list of books you want to read— books about writing, books like the ones you want to write someday, books that other writers seem to be reading and loving—there are lots of lists of books. Create your own schedule.*

ON YOUR PAGE: *Exercise 3*

Find a writing group that is open to beginners. You might place a "Wanted: Brand New Writers" ad at a local library. Many bookstores host manuscript exchange groups. Do you need to form a writing group? Learn how to give and receive responses to work? See the appendix for resources you can use to help you build these skills.

ON YOUR PAGE: *Exercise 4*

If you aren't ready for a writing group yet, simply attend live readings. Today, take some time to find out where such things are held in your time zone. Look on the Web, call bookstores and local colleges. Most schools and some museums have regular visiting writers series.

ON YOUR PAGE: *Exercise 5*

If you are terribly shy, terribly new, or you live in a truly isolated area, you can develop your public writer self skills by reading literary magazines, writing letters to authors whose works you adore, renting videotapes of writers reading their works aloud, listening to CDs of poets and storytellers and inviting people over to enjoy them with you.

ON YOUR PAGE: *Exercise 6*

As a writer, you aren't ever alone. In a fifteen-minute writing session, write down all the voices that are present in that session—books you can conjure up, teachers whose advice lingers in your head, writers in your community (no matter how famous or not, accessible or not), books on your shelves. What all around you, in your secret inner writing space, is noisy and full of writing energy? Write it all down.

Tips for Success

To develop your secret writing self:

1. Do exercises for writers instead of just reading them.

2. Stop talking about your writing, how hard it is, what you are doing, and your dreams. Instead, write.

3. Make a space in your life—a physical box house—where no one can enter. It can be as simple as a notebook you carry around, a special pen, a time of day.

4. Practice being quiet. Let other people talk. Listen, like you did when you were a kid, and you openly stared and absorbed everything. Be quiet. Leave some room in yourself for words to reverberate.

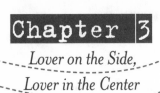

Chapter 3

Lover on the Side, Lover in the Center

IS YOUR WRITING LIFE GOING TO BE A LOVER IN THE CENTER of your life? The thing you pulse toward, the fever in your soul?

Or is your writing life more of a casual crush, something you think about, but don't do much about?

You know how when you are in love, lying with your lover, time stops—goes so fast and doesn't move at all? You feel mushy and goopy, and you are wet and hot and cool and loved and lovely, all at the same time.

Love: the great yumminess of life.

How many can you juggle at a time? Having a lover is a very time-consuming, distracting thing. Love and its pursuit can even be a pain in the butt. I have spent many, many novels worth of writing time chasing lovers, enchanting lovers, capturing and releasing lovers, crying over lovers, trying to make lovers into the people I want them to be. I have spent a lot of time yanking lovers into the center of my life. I often wish I spent more of my day writing. They're very alike: chasing the writing life, chasing the loving life.

Loving.

Writing.

What gives?

Not being busy. That is the greatest, most fearless act we can commit. That is a way of thanking, praising God for ensouling us. Being, and not distracting ourselves with the illusion of the power that is busy.

It feels so good to be busy—"I'm having a crazy day, I'm crazed, I'm so stressed, oh the schedule." I will never again utter those words. When I hear my friends utter this demon's curse, I smile and step back a teensy bit.

"Are you swamped?" my colleague Nat likes to ask me.

I always force myself to say no. I am not swamped. Why would I get swamped? That is not my life.

For me, it's too passive, too fake, too braggy to be always saying how busy I am. "I wish I had two more weeks before the semester starts," my boss says every summer in late August. I feel like we're feeling really insecure and unimportant when we talk like this. "I'm so important. I have been entrusted with so much work, there aren't enough hours in the day for me. Look at me! So much work!"

Get real, I want to say to my "busy" friends. Be accurate and tell the truth. You do have two weeks before school started. You do have time. Get a grip. Time is not all that surprising. If you can't do a whole lot more stuff, it's okay to just know that, and to stop orienting yourself in kinky ways to time. (See the appendix for good books on getting adult about time.)

Here's the thing. There is one way to make time stop. And only one way: Fall in love.

When you have a lover or a baby, you fall out of time, and into the beloved. Love is the only time in our lives when we are out of time.

To create a writing life, you will need to fall in love—deeply, seductively, passionately—with your writing life. It will become not a habit or a job, but a lover. If you keep it a second-string lover, your back-up lover, your Tuesday night sex-as-friends kind of lover, it might always be cranky with you. But if you make your writing life so lovely you can't take your eyes off it, you will space out during meetings, and dream about it as you go through the day, just like when you're in love.

Notice time.

Notice your passion.

Follow where those two intersect.

There is time in your day for writing—no matter how busy/important/stressed you are. You might not like me for saying this, but you do have twenty-four hours to spend. Same as everyone else. You can stop time by falling enormously in love with your own writing self. But your fear, your constriction, your no-saying will chase the love away. If you keep saying, "You're not good enough for me," that lover will stop calling you, stop bothering. If you keep saying that to your writing life—you're not important enough to me—the urge will die. Maybe slowly, but it will go away. Since that is what you have ordered it to do.

Some people get this message only when banged on the head.

Have you noticed God trying to get your attention lately? Have you fallen flat on your face—literally? My friend Ann, last Monday, had a very surprising day: Driving to school in her little station wagon, she had a flat tire. Then during her first lecture that morning, she lost a very painful, messy, awful tooth—there was blood. Lots. At the dentist she decided the pain was too much, and she cancelled her afternoon classes. She never does this. She went home and got in bed. Just as she pulled the covers over her head, pulling the cat to her for comfort, her bed broke. It crashed down onto the floor, with Ann and all her books and her cat and her aching raw gums.

Going too fast (your tires blow)? Biting off more than you can chew (teaching too many classes)? Not getting enough sleep (improperly repurposing your bed)?

A lot of writing books say, "Carve out fifteen minutes in the morning." "Write every night before bed." "Make a schedule."

I do not believe in those methods; they never work for me. Instead, I watch my life and follow my heart.

I listen for clues—now that I have been practicing this I can usually see the signs before major dental work is required.

I treat my writing life like a fabulous, enchanting lover, because that is what it is to me. Something that is terribly time consuming, delicious, and time-stopping. I have missed important meetings for love, and I will continue to put my writing life in the same position. My writing life is the lover at the center, not the neglected cranky demanding millstone, my ball and chain.

When you are in love, truly and passionately, you don't have to write down in your daily schedule *Spend quality time with Lover today.* You can't not.

And that's the secret to a happy writing life.

Having a writing life is like having a fabulous lover. You find yourself not paying bills on time, not showing up for boring things, spacing out during tedious conversations. Why would you go anywhere else? When you are loving, you are magnetized to the Source (God, love, whatever *it* is).

People who are madly in love are not busy. They spend inordinate amounts of time in hotel rooms, lolling around, naked, happy, content to look at the mole on their lover's neck and think about nothing at all.

They get hungry, but they aren't able to plan to eat. They pulse toward food, all thorax, no head, they are fed, they go back to bed. So happy. Not on schedule.

Can you have a lover on the side? What kind of personality do you have? Do you need to fully commit, order your priorities, track it all out: this many hours for baby Alyssa, this many for husband Frank, this many for food-gathering and feeding, this many for work, this many for writing life.

Can you be the writer you want to be (do you know what kind that is yet?) if it's always off to the side? Can ya cheat? Go visit him once in a while and know he will be happy to see you? Does your writing self feel fed that way?

Successful happy writers are the ones who carry the writing around with them all the time. No matter where they are. In the boardroom, during the PowerPoint presentation, they are playing back the movie from the night before—a line of a poem, a paragraph from the novel, a few words that keep banging up against each other. There's no choice, and no schedule. They are always in love, they are always doing it, they are always in writing. As in love.

It takes a lot of trust, to fall back into pleasure, to know it will always be there.

Every time you tell the world you are busy, you are saying to the universe: I need busy work because I am afraid. You are telling us that you like being busy. You are saying to the rest of us: Stay back a little bit. Don't come over to my house tonight. Who wants to be around the swamped? No one. It's safe. It's a protection.

You are saying: I am unhappy; I am afraid of my power. You are saying to us, to yourself: I am important and in a hurry and people just don't understand how good I am, especially me.

You, angel baby, are grooving on the busy drug. You are addicted to distraction. Like heroin, it feels so good the first time. The first time you had that busy day, you rushed and fled from task to person to event—you flew, you were so much like a fairy tale person, and look what got done!

Many of us spend the rest of our lives trying to re-create that busy buzz.

Which is fine. It is. Busy is an *interesting* lover. He will certainly fill up your center, the center of your life. You will not be lonely, not with Busy as your lover. You will feel the illusion of strength and power. And you will feel the hollowness that underlines all illusions of strength and power.

If you choose him, Busyness, as your lover, you must promise not to complain about your choice.

When you complain about your choice, you are pushing away people/love/your hopes/your dreams/happy accidents/insights/money—everything that is good, everything that you want. You are pushing it away.

Better lovers may be trying to locate you, knocking on your door. If you even hear, you are saying by your actions and by your complaining: I Am Freakin' Taken, Can't You See That?

When you groove on the busy drug, you are qualifying yourself, perhaps, for a job you don't want.

Take Lily, for example. Lily is in graduate school in social work. She has a cool husband, Joe, a house in the mountains, and a pregnancy she is beyond excited about.

She takes classes and teaches them—the regular graduate student life. She works in the summer on editing this and reviewing that. She really hates all this work, she says.

"What do you want to do?" I asked her when we met at a conference, and she was complaining the exact same complaints as the last time I met her.

"I want to write. I want more time for my writing!"

I was surprised to hear Lily say she wants to write. I am used to people saying to me they want to write *if only they had the time.* (I always look up to the sky, and check in with the gods when I hear this. *We all get the same amount of time, right?* "Yup," say the gods. "You mortals all get the same allotment. It's the single fair thing in life." "Thanks," I say. "Just checking.")

But Lily keeps herself so busy—is a writing life really what she wants?

Yes. Lily has a dream. She wants to be a writer. She wants to write fiction and nonfiction and poetry. The life she wants looks very different from the life she has—and loves.

She says yes to lots of things that have nothing to do with her dream. But they sustain the illusion—this is a powerful drug, remember—that she is working toward her dream. If only she weren't so busy.

Lily is so terrified of falling in love with her writing that she is doing everything in her power to keep writing-as-lover at a safe distance. And it's working!

It's quite the convenient trap.

Take Ron, another example. Ron wants to be a visiting writer at a university where he has an office, a few loyal students, and time to pen his novels. But while in graduate school, Ron spent enormous amounts of time publishing his work in any magazine that would take him. Ron has accrued hundreds of publications in places no one has ever heard of. He edited anthologies and worked on literary magazines. He helped students form a union to increase their wages in campus jobs. He raised rare and strange animals in fairly large quantity, and he moved a lot.

When Ron searched for a cushy slot as a university visiting-writer-in-residence, he was angry that his only job offer came from a small school in the middle of (to him) nowhere. The requirements of this job? Edit the student literary magazine, serve on committees, teach lots of classes. Hang around with the students. Publishing in gobs of tiny magazines would be an appropriate way to get ahead in this position.

Ron spent all his time qualifying himself for one job, the one job he didn't want! Employers look at his resume and say: "Perfect! A man who will do tons of stuff for our school, our students, and the local humane society, too!"

No one looked at Ron's application and said: "This guy looks like our next cushy visiting-writer-in-residence."

No one is going to come over to Lily's house and say to her: "Honey, sweety, you are such a hard worker. Spend the summer writing. Take four months, write your dream. Write your ass off. I want you to do that."

Lily and Ron are afraid, and unsure, and distracted. They are insecure—they "go out" with lots and lots of writing projects (inappropriate to their goals). They are afraid of committing to the demanding, fabulous, sophisticated, delicious superior love that is the Writing Lover.

Maybe you are, too.

Which takes us directly back to Question One. Can you

have a lover on the side? Can Lily write in the interstices, between the editing, the class preps, the social work conferences, and anthologies?

Hell, yeah!

She sure can. She is a completely strong, together person. Lily can do anything she wants. I have seen her—she climbs mountains, camps, does all kinds of mighty things I would never dream of doing.

But she first has to see the simple truth. Lily (says she) *wants* the writing to be her lover at the center. But she is doing everything in her power to date and court and bed on an hourly basis everything *but* the writing. She's hooked on an illusion, an excuse as addictive as crack cocaine, the busy drug.

The writing lover is saying the same thing to Ron: "What would you do with me? If you had me, how would you treat me? Would I just sit in the living room while you hurtled through this kind of odd life that doesn't even really make you that happy? I don't think I want that," the writing lover says. "I could maybe be your lover on the side, while you take care of your wife and the pets you love, but you'd have to stop complaining about being busy, because that would make me feel really strange—to be on the side, when you don't even love what you do keep in your center."

That's what the writing lover says. Love whatever is in first position, and quit complaining about it. If writing is your side action, own up to it. Have reasonable expectations about how much pleasure anything on the side can bring.

You can have your life's work—whatever that is, family, faith, a calling—in the center, and you *can* have a lover (the writing-life lover) on the side. You truly can, and you don't have to be French, alternative, wildly sexy, or younger or older. You don't have to look like someone from the movies and own expensive massage oils and silk thongs.

You pick.

That's all you have to do.

You have to pick.

And then support that choice with every fiber of your being—aka stop complaining.

No one has any more or less than you do. Talent, time, connections. Youth, money, computer equipment—those don't matter.

To write, you need so very little.

You need an honest heart. And some paper.

You need to approach your writing life just as you would a romantic partner, not as you would a discipline.

When you commit to lots of busy-making things *other people could truly do perfectly well,* are you popping power drugs? Are you doing a frenzied kind of scary dance in the center of your life to take up the emptiness there?

Are you sick of saying you want a writing life, more time for writing, when you keep not doing anything about it?

Choose what you want to be in the center.

Sit down, and quit thinking you are the center.

Make your center an inviting place. Stop complaining.

If you have the energy and are practiced in the ways of love, put writing in the center, just as you would a new lover, the love of your life. If you are committed already, take on writing as a lover on the side.

Let yourself be as passionately pulled to this lover as you would with an affair of the heart.

Time will fall away.

Love is the only way to create time.

I know this: You will be happier and you will make the people around you happier if you "shut up and sit down." Make it seem like you are at least choosing your own life. No one is really buying this idea that all these people are rushing up to you begging you to take on additional work. For some of you that is true, you are truly important people making life-changing decisions on a daily basis. Those of you who are actually important, you should just keep doing what you are doing.

If you want to write, stop qualifying yourself for every other job that is not writing.

You need to search for more areas in which you are under-qualified.

That is humbling, isn't it?

Lover in the center, lover on the side.

You decide.

ON YOUR PAGE: *Exercise 7*

As you read this chapter, it's likely that you said to yourself, "Fine, Heather, but I'm *XYZ* and I have *PDQ* going on, and in addition, the special circumstances of *ABC*." Good! Perfect! This is the right book for you!

The excuses you are making right now are illusionary distractions—and very, very useful. We need to write them down and look at them. So, do that. Write down what you were thinking—to-do lists, jobs, fears, dreams, excuses, busy-drugs you are addicted to, meetings you must attend, children you must feed. Write it all down. Look at your list. What job are you qualifying yourself for? What is at the center of your life? Are you in the mood to fall in love with writing? Are you too exhausted to take on a lover? Are you feeling like you should take on this lover, writing? Or do you really want to? Write out the answers to these questions.

Note: If you are so busy you can only do this exercise in your head, not writing it down, return this book to the store.

ON YOUR PAGE: *Exercise 8*

Set a writing schedule for the week. For example, 7 A.M. to 7:15 A.M., and lunch, and Saturday afternoon. Now, here is the key part: Nap during those hours. Do nothing. Just sit there, lie about, stare out the window. Be in bed. Or on your back. For one week. Waste your writing time. It's a lover. It needs that kind of mindless spending of time, that luxury of *wasted hours*. This is an excellent method for proving that you are deserving and worthy of a writing love. I think you will be surprised at the results! If you can't waste this amount of writing time, how will you write during it?

ON YOUR PAGE: *Exercise 9*

Take books to your bed. See the appendix for authors that are wonderful to sleep with. Get in the habit of reading in bed. Read every self-help book you can get your hands on. Watch your resistance to new ideas. Court the writing life by simply reading. That's wooing, you know. Quiet, elegant, sitting still in the center of your life. Reading is a fabulous way to seduce a writing practice into your life. Read naked. Read indiscriminately.

Chapter 4
Tools 101

ONE REASON I BECAME A WRITER INSTEAD OF A VISUAL artist is because a tube of cerulean blue cost $4.39.

I had four dollars, but I needed it for Budget Gourmet, which, at $1.99 a pop, made for cost-effective eating.

Writing takes only a few tools.

Much of it you can do it in your head.

Paper and pencil are for us enormous refinements, inventions that saved the word. We are a simple tribe.

As a beginning writer here is what you do *not* need:

Fancy blank journals

Expensive computer software

Anything new

Office supplies

An expensive education

Writers don't need anything that costs money, except paper and pencils (which are as cheap as Budget Gourmet). As you get established in your daily writing practice, fabulous add-ons, which people can buy you for your birthday, include paper clips and notebooks (in which you can store all your handwritten glorious pages).

What a life!

The tools a writer really needs are free. Hard-won, but free:

1. The ability (gets better with practice, just like anything) to spend time alone in your room writing on your paper with your cheap pencil.

2. Self-knowledge (the ability to see your own mental weirdnesses and bad thinking habits).

3. Access to a library. (Many libraries will mail books to your home!)

4. An observant heart. (Everyone is born with this item.)

You can practice acquiring larger quantities of the items on the above list all the time, even when you are being paid to do other things!

This chapter could be called "How to Make the Writing Not Grim" because my friend Ann says this is the best thing, maybe, about my workshops and writing classes. I know how to make the writing pleasurable and simple. We get our work done, and there's joy (yes!) in the whole process.

I get so tired of hearing writers complain about how hard it is to write. How hard it is to find the time to write. How hard it is to get published.

Complain about *anything* else.

Writing is a luxury. You do have the time to write (work on your mental habits). You do have the ability to write (work on your writing practice), and you will get published—you just will—if you write every day for long enough. Time and publication aren't what successful writers worry about it.

Having the right tools is what working artists worry about, and rightly so.

Three things to make writing something you do, not something you dread:

1. Stop complaining.

2. Write about what you want to write about.

3. Don't think about it.

All the time people are telling you what to write, what not to write. Magazines are telling you, simply by what they publish. Your stories/poems/essays/whatevers—no one is going to come over and say, "Honey, could you please, please write whatever you want, make it as long or short as you want, just write?"

No one is coming by your house to tell you that.

No one is leading you to your chair.

One of your important tools is your writing topics. You already have all these. They're in you. They always have been.

When Marianne Moore first started publishing her poems about flowers, the people who ran the poetry world were disdainful.

"Extraordinarily superficial," they said, all snooty and weird.

T.S. Eliot stuck up for Marianne Moore, saying, "Gentleman, excuse me, you write about what you write about. Why can't she?"

We all get to write about whatever the heck we want to write about.

I am always telling my students to write about their actual real topics, the things only they can tell us about. "You have great material!" I cry. I tell Wendy to write about her family's convenience store in St. Regis Falls, New York. I want Dana to stop writing about London (where she hasn't actually ever been) and to write about her apple orchard, and her wild and terrible year as a nanny in Switzerland. And Chris's cool psychotherapist parents are clamoring to be written about. Owen writes about parties really well—he can keep writing about parties. Tom, my student who is an eye surgeon, writes about eyes. Write about what is in front of your face. Or, in Tom's case, on your face.

Just tell us: Exactly what is it like, moment by moment, at breakfast with the girlfriend's parents and little sister and you are hungover? In the midmorning, in the gauzy light in the orchard? Getting into the car? Being in your aunt's house? This is what we want to know. The tiny things people do. The little things they say.

We want you to take five minutes from real life, and take five pages to write about it.

Again, and again, and again. We want to see in. Just for ourselves, without a lot of commentary from you.

My students don't want to write about St. Regis Falls and Hill Valley Orchard and their doctor's office and goofy stoic Dutch ancestors.

Write what you want to read, I remind them.

You can't expect all the other writers to reveal their secrets and tiny details while you hoard yours.

Isabel Allende says again and again that writing is joyous and easy and happy and free.

It's the best thing we do for ourselves. It's like eating right and sleeping. It's a natural, easy, lovely part of the day. What could be cozier than you, sitting at your desk, writing?

We *make* it really complex.

We analyze it to death.

We think we need tools—software and filing cabinets and degrees and high-powered critique groups and paid-to-read editors-for-hire. We think we need to live in New York or on an island. We think, most of all, we need more time.

Just sit down.

You have all the tools you need.

Right here, right now.

Write in the back of this book!

Write.

It's just you, words, paper (or computer screen). It's not a big deal.

I think sometimes we secretly wish it were a bigger deal. Is that why we block?

It's just flowers?

Well, I know—writing is not that simple and easy to do. The other day I was in the bookstore with my husband and kids. Jacob sat reading a book in a big comfy bookstore chair. David Junior was pacing about the T-shirts and caps, trying everything on. He is fourteen and enjoys looking at himself in the mirror.

David the dad had one small book, a book of meditations. I came galloping up to the counter to meet him.

I had in my arms exactly fourteen books.

He smiled.

"Oh," I said. "I wasn't going to buy any. I know. Hey, help me cull, help me get rid of some of these. Okay?"

"Ya sure?" he said. He is very hesitant to give anyone criticism, direction.

"I am sure. You tell me if I really need this book."

"Okay," he said. He held up *Paula*, a memoir by Isabel Allende.

He said, "Good one. You sure you don't have it?"

"Pretty sure," I said. I put it by the register. The keep pile.

Then he lifted up the two self-help books on simplicity. "Honey," he said. "You already have a lot of books like this."

"I do, don't I?" I looked at the books. One was a program where you can make one modification in your life every week for eight weeks. I liked the promises—you'd be leaner, cleaner, and more creative in two months.

"You're already doing the exercises in that running book, and you're talking about the women's creativity group thing, and you've got *Aha! 10 Ways to Free Your Creative Spirit and Find Your Great Ideas* going, too. I saw it on the bedside table."

"Oh, yeah, I did start that program. I forgot. I have all these programs going." (The simplicity movement has a very complex, very consumer side to it, if you haven't noticed.)

I put back all the self-help books. I put back *Paula* because I wasn't sure if I already owned it or not.

I bought a book on architecture to read with the kids. And I bought a book by Guy Davenport on how to look at paintings.

[*Note*: I have not, as of this moment (twelve months have passed), read either of these two books.]

I love self-help books and books on writing.

But, David is completely right. I do not need more of these books—they clutter up my life and make me feel I'm not creative enough, thin enough, clean enough, organized enough, helpful enough, intuitive enough, spiritual enough, woman enough, man enough, fit enough, etc. They make me feel I need to improve. That is not simple.

It's the opposite of simple.

The single most important tool in your tool kit is to stay simple—truly simple. Stop making this harder than it is.

Yes, it takes constant checking to make sure your head isn't getting in the way of your writing practice. But that's it!

You already know everything you need to know. You do not need any more tools. You do not need charts or storyboards or rhyme schemes or shortcuts. You do not need vows, resolutions, rules, classes, or a program.

You know everything you need to know.

You need to sit down every day and write.

The last thing you need to simplify your life is a book on how to simplify your life. These books, while important and interesting and filled with good ideas, end up making most of us feel bad. Additionally, they take up the very space we are supposed to be clearing out.

It's like looking at the Pottery Barn catalog or Garnet Hill or mass magazines of just about any ilk. You look around at your own house, and you see the extension cords and the outlets and the stuff (you don't see any real life in those catalogs), and you feel like your house is a messy (though electrified) disaster. This is sad.

You live in your house—it's your house. You need to love your house. Just as it is. Stop looking at false advertisements for real life and for a writing life that doesn't even exist. Stop feeling like your writing life doesn't have "enough"—enough time, enough space, enough quiet, enough cool stuff. That's an illusion and you need to just stop it. Love your writing life! It's your writing life. And I promise, if you show up for your twenty minutes of daily practice, you'll feel very rich indeed.

To write, you need to simply write.

The tools of your trade are in you.

Don't make it harder than it is.

Sit down in your chair. And write. Don't think. Take your day yesterday, and pick a moment—a moment when other people were around. When you first woke up, or when you got to work, or lunch. It doesn't matter which moment. Freeze frame this moment by doing a little sketch on your paper: Who was there? Draw a tiny *X* on the page for each person. What were they doing? Where was this? What time of day? What was going on in the background? At the top of your page, jot down your answers to those questions. Then, set your time for fifteen minutes.

You are going to write exactly what happened—no emotions, no adjectives—just what happened, in short simple sentences, trying to capture, exactly, every gesture, every bit of dialogue, every reaction. Just start, and play the scene out in your mind, like a movie, rewinding whenever you lose your place. Like this: "I'm at work, in the teacher's lounge. It's ten after eight. Kathy is drinking coffee at the table. Martha is running the copier, only she's talking, so nothing is happening, actually, with the copies. Joseph is leaning against the Coke machine. He says, 'Well, gals, did anyone see old Kit this morning?'"

Write like that, for the full fifteen minutes. Go slowly, and write by hand. You want to cover five minutes of real time in fifteen minutes of writing time. This is a good formula. It can be one of your writing tools, something to add to your kit.

Remember, you don't need to buy anything to be a writer. You just focus, and do it.

Chapter 5
Journals

I HATE THE PHRASE, "KEEPING A JOURNAL."

I like a loose journal, not a kept one.

Some beginning writers avoid the journal. I understand this—it's a cumbersome appendage. Dragging this half-empty book around, some of the pages scribbled with crap and drivel. It looks like homework. It smells of pretense. What do you write, anyway?

Why *would* you keep a journal?

I would like to present an alternative way of looking at the journal, so you, too, can incorporate the unheralded pleasure of note-taking into your writing life. I don't know a single working writer who doesn't lug around a notebook, or pop pieces of paper into a pocket or glove box. Writers, especially beginners, can't ever be more than two feet away from a piece of paper and a pencil.

My journal is full of spare words, extra bits of this and that. Loose change. My journal is promiscuous, loose, easygoing, easy to please, fun to have around.

Not kept. I don't *keep* my journal. I let it go. I don't worry about writing in it every day. I don't read it over, go back through it, stay in the lines, or set up any rules at all.

I never worry about finishing or filling a journal. I buy 'em, blank, all the time. No order or plan or program.

"Keeping" sounds restrictive to me, and orderly. I don't

like anything kept, really—kept woman, pets are kept, houses are kept, the soul beat right out of them. The word "kept" doesn't make me want to sit down and pour words on paper. It makes me want to hide, like I did from my mom when it was time to sweep the patio.

Journal keeping—it sounds like something you'd have to do if your job was to watch how many sips of water tiny mice took in thousands of cages under heat lamps or something.

"Keeping your journal, are ya?"

"Yupper, it's up to date."

Sounds like *a lot* of fun.

My journals are loosed, lost, unleashed, splashed upon the world. They do not make sense. I do not write in them regularly. I don't even know where they are half the time.

Sometimes I date the entries.

Most of the time they aren't entries, though.

I will go for weeks without writing in a journal.

A journal is meant to be something you have with you when you are not in your house, and you are bored, or grumpy, or staring off into space. This is when you write in your journal. On a trip, you write down what people are saying in the airplane seats behind you. Good use of the journal. You sketch the banana trees outside your hotel. You listen to your grandma's recipes for corn bread and grits, and you write them down in your journal, plus a description of her skin, her earrings, the wonderful way her hair wisps around in a circle. Good use of a journal.

Notes when you are reading. Writing exercises you *want* to try. Things you want to look up. Book titles you want to pursue. Cool quotes. Good for a journal.

My journal is a web, as in spider web, and I catch stuff I can use later in it. Lots of detritus of the day, too, gets stuck in the web. Things pass through it on their way into my stories, essays, and poems.

My journal has lists, snippets of conversations, descriptions, funny things kids say, words I like, words I need to look up, addresses and phone numbers of shops, people, grocery stores I want to visit more often. I tape in fortune cookie fortunes. Sometimes I draw, list scenes for a novel. I write mad letters I never mail anywhere. I write down how my day is or isn't going.

When I am bored at a church service or poetry reading, I jot, muse, dash, scribble.

A journal can't be a chore. Your journal has to be like wine or friendship or dessert or telephone conversations—free form, light, engaged, enriching, pleasant, attached.

There are so many great books on journals—nature journals, illuminated journals, making your own journals. Look in the appendix for more on this.

Your journal can be as complicated or simple, ugly or beautiful, playful or hardworking, as you want. This can even change from day to day. You need a journal, or at the very least, you need a little packet of paper of some kind that is always with you.

When you start writing daily, a funny thing is going to happen. You're going to have things you want to jot down, to feed into the next day's session. When you're grocery shopping or coaching Little League or helping your mom with her plants, stuff is going to come in. You need your paper, and you must write these things down, or imperil your own development as a writer. Ignore those flashes long enough, don't write them down, and they'll stop coming. Not what you want.

If you aren't the type to just compose words, ink flowing all over your clean white pages, you might try another trick. I like to jump-start my writing by keeping a pile of books and said journal by my bed on my nightstand. The books I keep with this journal (remember, I have about six journals going at any one time, no rules here) are books of writing exercises.

When I can't sleep or on weekend mornings when I feel like lying in bed and writing something, strengthening a few muscles, I get out one of my books of prompts. These are books written by teacher-type people, and they are filled with recipes for writing. And I use these books like cookbooks—paging through, reading whatever catches my eye, *Maybe I could do that one*, I'll think. I crook or flag the page. I keep reading through, planning fiction-feasts in my mind until I can't not write.

A journal keeps you going. It fertilizes your writing practice.

ON YOUR PAGE: *Exercise 11*

Buy a large journal, 8 ½" x 11", and keep it by your bed. You can also use a spiral bound notebook, for which you should pay no more than 99¢. When you can't sleep, or you are cranky and giving yourself a Time Out (it isn't just for kids!), or when you are stuck in your writing life, or just feel like writing, you can get it out, get it down. Tomorrow when you wake up, don't get out of bed without writing one sentence. Just one sentence. That's all.

Chapter 6
Sleeping With Books

I SLEEP WITH BOOKS.

In my bed, lots of books. A friend of mine says: If you have a pile of books in your bed, it means you need a lover in your life.

I like to have books in my bed.

I like to sleep with a person, too.

But I really like a lot of books in my bed.

When I make the bed, which I do rarely, books fall out, old copies of *The New Yorker*, an *Atlantic* or this morning, Marie Howe's new poems along with a little cascade of paperback short story collections.

With books, I am promiscuous.

You can't get too far off track as a writer if you are reading. In fact, I don't know any successful writers who don't read. Writers read. Reading completes the gesture. Reading is what we do. An enormous part of learning how to write better is learning how to read, sensitively, attuned to all the colors and emotions. In order to get better as a writer, you have to be able to read your own work, again and again and again. After a while, you learn how to listen for the clunky parts, the rich passages. The best way to tune your ear for this work is to read with passion and abandon.

You have to read widely. You have to read against your grain. Writers-in-training will want to read books they wouldn't normally read—the history of the pencil, biographies of seventeenth-century women, the night sky, bird books, historical novels. Writers suck up books. Keep reading what you love, but keep branching out. Isolate what you don't like to read, and read toward it, baby steps, tiny bites. Writers thrive on a diet of poetry, essays, novels, reference books, literary magazines. There's a whole food pyramid out there! At the base, books like the ones you are trying to write. At the very, very top, whatever comes most easy to you; the fats and oils are fantasy or beach books, writing books (!), or trashy tell-alls. It's vitally important that as a writer you read. Read books by writers from all over the world. Read African writers, Japanese writers, Peruvian poets. Read from all the centuries, browse, avoid trends, extend yourself.

My college boyfriend and I only had three rooms in our house. I was outgrowing the box house I'd built in the living room, and the bed was tiny and in the dining room, and he slept with books, too. So we moved to Milton Street, to a five-room house. I had my own bedroom in that little white-wood Southern frame house facing the street. And he had his. The dining nook had a table in it, instead of a bed. Milton Street was quiet and wide.

I bought an air conditioner for my room and set to nesting. I dragged in a mattress, a double, flat, old, worn mattress that took up most of the floor. In the margins, I piled books.

Clothes, books, a kayak paddle, a kite, and more, and more, and more books. As a student, I checked out dozens of books a week from the Florida State library. I was always thrilled when I found one that had never been checked out! I loved these books, ancient virgins, and I ferried them back to my lair with great care.

When I discovered professors could check out books from the library for the entire semester, I got a job working for an economics professor just so I could use his library privileges, and poach books, as it were.

As an undergrad I had a library card at my local public library. I thought everyone did. Later I realized most students don't go to the local library in their new town. I have never not had in my living room a pile of overdue art books, coffee-table books, cookbooks, bathroom books. From a range of libraries.

When I was a kid, I spent dozens of hours building houses with books and large Legos. It was my favorite thing to do with my brother. I built houses with garages, and working farms, and rocket-making annexes (for his aerospace businesses to operate), and I built them all out of books. Cantilevered houses were big in the seventies, and when I checked out books from the Orlando Public Library, I had one eye on content and the other eye on form. I liked a library binding (thick, single colored, blue-green matte, tough), and I liked size: books on art and architecture.

I also wanted something to read for when the building became monotonous, and my brother wanted to go outside and blow things up. As I disassembled my structures, I fell into reading.

Once my college boyfriend said, "You read a lot. It's a good thing about you."

And I was stunned. I was twenty-two and in school, and it only seemed like I had never, ever read enough and never would. "I do?" my insecure little self said to the Wise Older Boyfriend. "Really?"

"You read more than anyone I know."

My reading is a full-body experience. I bathe with books and they bloom, like peonies. I have my new Richard Ford hardback in there now, and the stories and the Swiss Foam Bath and the hot water mix together in a steamy decadent scrumptious love fest of reading.

I like to read, like Flannery O'Connor and Eudora Welty (women without husbands and children), in the morning, before I talk, before I write.

I have, in addition to the bed pile, piles of books by my bed, on my dresser, on my desk, on my dining room table, and in my car.

I leave books behind, in restaurants and hotels, on trains and buses, and in the homes of friends.

I write in my books. I always try to write in my journal about what I am reading, but I can't remember to always keep up with it; it feels like discipline, and I do best with a lot of freedom. So I write down what is happening in my mind as I read, write in the margins. To-do lists and love letters and notes to friends—it's all in the books I'm reading.

I have read through many evenings, dozens of weekends, vacations, summers, and entire relationships.

My reading is infused with the same kind of obsession I want my writing to maintain. It's all about ease, absorption, and falling into the dream state. I'm pulled that way. And I imagine productive writers are pulled to their writing the same way we are to books.

To discover or deepen your proper writing practice, I want you to think Love Affair.

I want you to make love to books!

Now, really imagine your writing life is a love affair. I want you to get out some paper and make a little love list. What kind of relationship are you having with your writing life?

Here's the note I wrote last week when I was in a really good relationship with my writing:

Can't wait to get to desk and be with novel.
Think about novel all day, and all night.
Write lots of notes to novel in margins of books, journal.
Make plans around novel instead of other way around, friends
*   can wait.*
Think novel is most wonderful thing in world.
Know novel and I understand each other better than anyone or any
*   thing else ever could. Definitely in love with novel these days.*

Now, you do it. What's your relationship like? List its features.

My reading life is always fabulous. I try to bring that same set of behaviors to my writing life. I read with abandon, I'm completely promiscuous with books. And when my writing life is how I want it to be, it's dominated by Lust and Ease. I don't mind being late to school or up too late writing—it's all I think about. Love, reading, a writing life—maybe they aren't supposed to be anything you have to think about too much. A healthy writing life: nothing like school and everything like passion. Even when you aren't doing it, you are happy because there is always something to think about, something next, something delicious and tempting and good.

When my writing life is not going well, my list is very different. We'll focus on that later. For now, if you can't think of how you treat your writing life on good days, write about when you are able to become completely absorbed by books (or another passion). Write about a time you were in such a state that you acted as though you had a new lover.

If there is no time like this in your life, you need to put this book down, go to your nearest bookstore or library, and get lost there. Go. Now.

Use/develop your passion for books as a way to develop your passion for getting lost in your own writing.

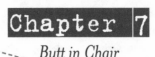

Chapter 7
Butt in Chair

SOMETIMES TEACHERS MAIL ME THEIR STUDENTS' REACTIONS to my readings or talks. One gal in Minnesota dutifully attended my lecture, and she listed out in her assignment— summarize the lecture—my topics.

"Sellers talked about the daily writing, her dogs, and the button chair method."

At first, I didn't know what this woman, Emily from Minnesota, who was getting extra credit for spending an hour on her Tuesday listening to me, meant. I had no idea. What was my button chair method?

A few days later, it came to me.

Butt in Chair! I had talked about Butt in Chair!

Someone had asked me a question during the talk in Minnesota. "What is the your best single piece of advice to the beginning writer?"

I said, "Butt in Chair."

Suddenly, I liked Emily's concept way better than my own.

You button your pants onto special hooklike features mounted on your desk chair. You've already set the timer, and you can't be unhooked from that chair until the time is up.

Button chair, Butt in Chair—regardless of how you spell it, the concept is an old one: You have to stay in your chair.

You can't do the laundry.

You can't clean things.

You can't take a bath, a shower, a walk.

You can't do any of the healthy necessary things you have been meaning to do: practice yoga, call your mother, write letters. All of those holy pure acts will seem appealing. You must resist bettering yourself in those ways.

You sit in the chair.

Whether or not you are writing.

Flannery O'Connor is famous for saying: "I don't know if the muse is going to show up or not on any given day, but by golly, I'm going to be at my desk from 8 to 12 every morning in case she does."

Are you willing to put up with a lot of (seemingly) wasted days, a lot of staring, a lot of being quiet by yourself? That's what real writers do. That is what you have to do. Practice the fine art of the Butt in Chair.

One writer calls it the "Talent of the Room." She means that you have to develop one talent alone as a writer, and it isn't, surprisingly, how to write sex scenes, how to create mind-bending plot, how to get published, how to meet and greet powerful agents. It's simple: It's the talent of sitting, in a room, by yourself, with no one but yourself, and just getting used to that.

Most people can't practice the Talent of the Room. They've never been taught. They've never noticed it matters.

Most people can't sit alone by themselves (again, this is why I love to have athletes and yoga practitioners in my writing classes, because they *do* know how to do this and have already practiced *a lot*).

Why not?

Well, there you are. You. All your demons and failings and

mind-chatter, and messiness. You think doing the laundry will cleanse you! You think if you keep moving you won't have to deal, listen, see, know. Or that you will anyway, and so why not get things picked up, the place is a disaster.

Sitting alone in a room by yourself is very hard.

Monks and nuns and prisoners write beautifully about how the skill can be variously mastered.

It's not for the faint of heart.

To develop the Talent of the Room, you need training in concentrating. You have to be able to focus, deeply, on one thing, in order to sit still long enough to write.

When you look inside your self—and you will look if you are left alone with yourself for more than fifteen minutes—you won't know how to love what you see, without practice, without training.

Patience.

A high tolerance for anxiety.

Skills for self-knowledge.

This is the skill that is called Butt in Chair.

Butt in Chair is how the writing gets done.

To develop a successful writing life you must be able to focus and concentrate. Start small. Use a timer—you are only *allowed* to focus on your writing for, at first, ten minutes. Use an egg timer—something that doesn't make noise. Write by hand (it's too easy to erase and too easy to go fast on the computer). Typewriters are good. Write exactly what you see in your mind's eye. Or write what you hear. There are a number of good books on what to do in your focused time (see the appendix). Lynda Barry teaches wonderful workshops using this method.

Here are the rules for focused writing time:

Write very slowly.

Write in all capital letters. (To distract your busy brain.)

Don't think and don't plan—write exactly what you see or hear.

Start at the beginning of your ten minutes and don't stop moving your pencil (or marker—pens slide too fast) until time is up.

Work up to fifteen minutes, then thirty. It is extremely hard to concentrate for thirty minutes. Most meditation tapes and sessions are twenty-two minutes, the side of a cassette tape.

As you seek master status, you can work up to forty-five minutes. Then, you'll need a break. Most writers I know can't do more than two hours of this kind of work in a day.

If you really have been concentrating, you will feel a number of things at the end of your session:

1. That time slipped away—that you weren't aware of time passing. Like when you are driving sometimes, and you arrive, and you have no memory of ever passing any of your usual landmarks—it's like you were in a time warp.

2. Pleasantly exhausted. You'll feel like you worked. You will feel tired, but in a good way, like you do after raking leaves or doing anything physical that's hard, but not too hard. You'll feel a sense of accomplishment.

3. Inclined to read your work over. Don't do this. You need to develop a habit of concentration, the Talent of the Room. If you end every session with a judgment, *oh, I'm so good and oh, I totally suck*, you won't keep doing this. I promise. Who would show up for daily judging? Yuck.

You are showing up simply to practice concentration. If you concentrated, you were successful. If you didn't, that's okay, because you are just practicing. Practice again tomorrow.

Do this ten days in a row, and your writing life will change. I can guarantee this.

ON YOUR PAGE: *Exercise 13*

How long can you sit? If you don't do this regularly, expect it to be one of the hardest things you've ever taken on. And, like archery, or swimming, or driving a car, it's easier to learn with a teacher, or a coach, than from a book. You are trying to learn *focus* and concentration. But you can practice on your own.

Butt in Chair. Work up to more time, each day. Work up to a ritual. That's all, really, you need to know about writing.

The fabulously inexpensive one-size-fits-all button chair.

For today, I want you to get a timer.

Get set up—you need plain unlined paper, a pencil, and a comfortable quiet place to be. Take some deep breaths in and out. Relax your body, as though you are trying to get ready for sleep.

Set the timer for three minutes. A noisy clanky timer won't work—the timer must be completely quiet—something you glance at. A watch that vibrates or any electronic beeping thing will work, but I like the hourglasses with sand the best.

Number your paper from one to ten.

Make a list of ten things you saw two days ago, starting from the morning and ending with night. Keep your hand moving. If you get stuck, draw slow circles. You want to end up at exactly number ten at exactly the end of three minutes. Don't write a novel at each item, just a few anchoring words to capture the image are all you need to put down. Like this:

Saturday, December 2
1. *8 a.m. the windows frosted in swirls*
2. *The dog food scattered on the porch*
3. *Lentil soup in old Pyrex refrig. dishes*
4. *Wet leaves in the gutter*
5. *Dog hair all over my husband's black pants in the van*

Three minutes. One list.

Then, set your timer for ten minutes. Look over your list. Let one item pick you, or, if nothing leaps out, do number three. Number three is magic and always works.

Write the item number and words at the top of a fresh sheet. Same rules: You must keep your pencil moving, you must write slowly, all caps, skipping lines. Write in simple clear sentences. Don't try to be fancy. Avoid adjectives and adverbs. Just write in nouns and verbs, very simply, very slowly.

For ten minutes. Write what you see. Write what you hear.

It's really hard!

Don't read it over; don't judge the work. This is the kind of foundational practice every writer must build in order to have a successful writing life.

Rituals are great for art.

Several writers I know do this method with a candle burning. Others play music. Others have a special pair of pajamas. Lots of writers do their concentration exercise in bed. I do.

You can practice focusing like this any time of day, any where. Always have your journal with you. I like Rhino Journals the best.

They are hard, and light, and the paper has the right tooth for slow concentrated writing and circle drawing.

In the dentist's office, waiting for your kid's basketball scrimmage to end, while the laundry is drying, when you are cranky and out of sorts—you can do ten minutes of concentrating any time. It's an amazing tool. I can't stress this enough.

You have to learn to concentrate and focus in order to write. You have to be able to conjure up the Talent of the Room. Use ritual. Use short assignments, and avoid critiquing and judging—you'll never make it that way. You have to simply find, for yourself, this incredible pleasure. You'll feel it. You'll get hooked on it. You'll *want* to go back to the room, soon.

Do this exercise—three minutes plus ten minutes—for ten days in a row.

Your life will change.

Chapter 8
The Russian Lady

LAST WEEKEND, I WAS SPEAKING TO A GROUP OF LIBRARY patrons in West Palm Beach. I was on a panel with three other writers. It was me, a novelist, a nonfiction writer, and a memoirist. The hall was filled with men and women—mostly retired. This audience was *listening*. You could see they cared a lot about books.

We writers read and talked, and then it was time for the audience to ask questions.

In the tenth row was a woman, seventy years old, maybe older. She wore a beautiful long-sleeve burgundy dress. She had deep red hair. She looked very elegant, and wealthy and strong.

She stood up. "I was born in Russia," she said, in an old and powerful accented voice. Her words filled the room. She was the first person up. I thought: *How brave.* I also thought: *Please don't talk for a really, really long time.*

She said, "I was born in Russia, and it was very, very difficult. I have a story. Do I write it? My friends all say to me to write this down."

I held my breath. People don't want to hear. I was worried for the Russian Lady. I was worried she was going to tell us all this story. Lots of people come to writing conferences with a story they don't know what to do with. They tell it, a lot. It's like fishing. They are hoping for a tug, a nibble, something to yank on their line. I think they are secretly hoping (aren't we all?) someone will say, "You must write this book, and here, I will show you exactly how, calling you every day to make sure you're getting the support you need to write this book." They tell the story, at length. They don't write it at all.

But then, she only said this: "What should I do?"

And I was reaching for the microphone, when the writer next to me on the panel took it. I was about to tell the Russian lady I was sure she did have a story to tell, and it was no doubt an important one. I was about to say there are books available on how to write that story, good books such as Dan Wakefield's *The Story of Your Life* and Denis Ledoux's *Turning Memories Into Memoirs*. I was about to tell the Russian lady to just start, and do a little every day, and write down everything she could remember, a little at a time, to stick with it—my usual cheer-leading routine.

The writer next to me was thirty-seven years old. His book, a novel, was just out, and it was a huge success. He lived in New York City. He was dressed in black. He looked like an expensive kitchen knife, cutting his way neatly through pastel, sleepy West Palm Beach. With the microphone in his hand, he said, "A book is a lot of work."

I was thinking, *Oh, this is a bit mean, perhaps a tiny little bit rude—we need to encourage stories. We need her story. She needs to write it. We mustn't dampen the spirits of the new writer, even if, especially if, she is seventy-five years old.*

But the hip young writer said, leaning over our table, his voice soft, "My book took years for me to write. It was really, really hard. It was all consuming. Do you want to write your story? Or do your friends just want you to? You have

[64]

to decide. Do you want to embark on a long, hard project? Maybe you do. But maybe you don't. Listen to yourself. Not your friends."

In that moment, something changed in me.

I have always been telling everyone to write, write, write. That is what saved my life. It's not the same for everyone.

In my efforts to make myself write more, more, more, I have not been paying attention to what is right for you. Right for the Russian Lady, right for my student Sarah, with her eating disorder and cute boyfriend, right for my tormented closet-poet colleague.

Hence, this book.

Its mission: to help you clarify for yourself what you want, how you want to be in your life, what you want to spend your time thinking about and making and writing (or not writing).

Writing is a ton of work. It's exhausting. You can hardly do it when you are tired—it's that hard to do well. It's a way of life, and you have to really look hard inside yourself. It's like cleaning house—fun to have finished, less fun to do. Writing is not always the answer. It's not always right to say to people: "Yes, you have a great story. You should write it."

Maybe you should write. Maybe not.

Are your friends telling you to write? Do they know what's involved with that?

Are you feeling you *should* write? Why?

You don't have to write. You might not write. We don't want you stuck in a neurotic loop, lingering, looping, saying, "I am going to write my story just as soon as _____ (insert excuse here: I get more time, I retire, I get a job, I have kids, I don't have kids, etc.)."

The question posed to the Russian Lady is a great one. Do you want to write?

Do you?

If you write a long project—a book—you won't see as much of your friends as you are used to. Writing a book is hard.

It's really, really hard. It takes an ability to focus. What is the right focus for you? How will you find out? Is writing your story the best way for you to tell it?

Does a writing life work in your life?

To have a writing life you have to do two things: Withdraw, focus. These are really hard for most people.

My friend Kate is a fantastic poet. When she isn't writing, she has gall bladder attacks, migraines, irritable bowel. It's as if all those words get stuck in her, and wreak havoc on her system.

On the other hand, you don't have to write.

Maybe it isn't your dream.

Maybe someone else thinks you should write, and they tell you to write—like the Russian Lady. Do you want to write? What is right, for you?

If you are supposed to write, go ahead. Do it. Not writing *might* make you sick.

If you are supposed to write, stop thinking about it. Definitely stop talking about it.

Do you need to write? You can take a year off from the whole question, not think about it once, and then you'll know for certain. Decide to not write for a year—joyously, intentionally. No writing for you. Will you miss it? Will not feeling like you have to write—that story your sister wants, the autobiography of your mother, your husband's genealogy, your novel—free you up for other things? The things you were truly meant to do?

You don't have to write.

You also don't need to analyze much about writing. Get up, sit down at your desk, and put words on the page.

If you are a writer, you write stuff down, every day. If you aren't a writer, you can have lunch with your friends, tell long stories about your life and odd people you know—just because you are good at storytelling doesn't mean you should become a writer!

Listen to your friends when they tell you ruffled blouses aren't for you. Listen to your friends when they tell you that you are magnificent in purple, that the white tuxedo is pure good on you. When it comes to writing, only you know what is right for you. Only you. Sometimes people tell us to write a book when really they just want to read one. Sometimes they tell us to write a book because they themselves wish they had our experiences, our stories. Sometimes, I am sad to say, they tell us to write a book because they don't want to listen so much. Lots of times people say, "That would make a great story!" when they really mean, "That sure was interesting!" You don't want to revise your entire life and see way less of your children and friends based on *that*.

Here are a few exercises to help you decide what is really *right for you* right now.

ON YOUR PAGE: *Exercise 14*

Write down anything you can think of that people have told you would make a great book or story. Your childhood in the Philippines, your autistic sister, your ability to throw fantastic children's birthday parties ... anything you have in your life that anyone has said would make great material. Now, in your journal write out the question:

Do I really want to write about _____?

Expand on your answer. Why don't or do you? What do you want to write? Do you want to write, really, or are you most interested in having books with your name on them that you point to? Do your friends want you to write more than you need to write?

Just write, for ten minutes or so, and ask yourself these questions. Be gentle and polite with yourself.

Reminder: You can't do these exercises in your head and get the same results.

Maybe what you really want is to have someone else write it.

Maybe you want, really, to be interviewed.

Maybe you want to paint, instead.

Maybe you just want to have lunch with your friends, and talk.

ON YOUR PAGE: *Exercise 15*

Ten minutes, in your journal: Write about your unwritten projects. Interview yourself and find out what it is you really want to write. Ask yourself questions, the same ones you'd ask a Famous Writer on a panel. What is your next book going to be about? What projects must you get to before you die? What themes have developed in your work over the decades? (Pretend you are very prolific, very adored, and very famous, in the high-middle of your fabulous career.) Ask yourself anything!

ON YOUR PAGE: *Exercise 16*

Write down titles—first thing that pops into your mind—for the following books by you:

A poem about your worst winter

A children's book about two dogs

A memoir about your mother

A biography about you in your midlife

A novel set in your hometown

A book of your collected wisdom

A mystery novel with a surprising child detective at its center

ON YOUR PAGE: *Exercise 17*

If you want to write a book, take fifteen minutes—no more than that—to write a description of that book. If you're stuck, read a few jacket-flap paragraphs on books you have at home on your shelves or on the backs of paperbacks in the library. Don't think, just write down the brilliant evocative praise your book will receive. You might start with the following:

> "Rich, strange, and alive with the miracles of daily life, this novel is a banquet for the soul."

Or:

> "(Title of your novel here) is hilarious and at the same time desperately sad. Full of wit and poetry and exquisitely observed perceptions of the human condition."

Or:

> "A lighthearted romp through ..."

ON YOUR PAGE: *Exercise 18*

Take a few minutes to think about some of the motivations for your writing. Why do you want to write? How often do you write? Is someone else telling you to write? Should he or she be writing? Start like this:

> I need to write because ... (write for ten minutes).
> I don't need to write because ... (write for ten minutes).

Tips for Success

Writing is a big commitment. It's like training for a marathon. If you don't really want to complete a marathon—if the things you enjoy are picnics and movies and watching golf on television—you probably won't sign up for a marathon training program at your local sporting goods store. The same for writing. If you don't want to develop the ability to focus (really hard to do) and commit to a daily writing program (at least two hours, maybe four, for at least one year, maybe more), then you don't have to! I give you permission to revise your dream. Look over the work you did in this chapter (you have to write it out, these exercises can't be done in your head). What kind of person do we have here? Does this person want to write? Maybe not that much. It's okay not to be a writer. Sometimes when we say, "You should write that!" we really just mean, "Thanks for sharing that great story with me." And nothing more has to happen. At all. Ever.

Chapter 9
The Rents

I LEARNED THIS EUPHEMISM, "RENTS," FOR "PARENTS," FROM my students, and I'm happy to have it now in my own personal lexicon.

The rents. Taking the "pa" out of "parent." I like it. (Students are brilliant co-creators of the language, it's a sensual, live force to them, and more adults should listen, just listen to teenagers because the language is very alive in these people. Less correcting and judging, and more listening and enjoying!)

Oh, the rents. The rents are just that—they rent space in you.

It's good to have occupied space—you don't want a lot of empty space just sitting there—you'll get squatters, unwanted pests, dry rot (that is, addiction, depression, television?). The rents are fine renters ... *if* you are aware that they are renters and capable of everything renters are capable of, nothing more, nothing less. What happens to most of us is we forget they are in there. We forget they are capable of making structural changes!

The subject of this chapter is how your parents help define your writing life—whether you want them to or not. You have to shine a little light on them, I believe, as you carve out that joyous free writing life.

Let's take a peek.

The reason you write—or don't write—has something to do with your parents.

You don't need to analyze your parents. But you do have to be aware of your own hardwiring if you are going to weather the storms of the writer's life. The hardest thing to do as a writer, as I am hoping you know by now, is to develop a practice that you come to every day. To devise a way to deal with the inevitable forces and voices that say: *Don't write, it's not worth it, you can't, not you.*

What did your parents tell you about artists? What do they think about people who sit quietly in a room alone? What about people who love reading books? Or writers? What do they really think, your parents?

This might be different from what they say. What do your parents really think about people who tell the truth, even when it hurts? What was their relationship to writing? Was it one of longing? Indifference? Both? Something else? In your culture, who gets to be a writer, and how does the writer claim this life? Your parents have some important answers to these questions.

I write because my parents are both writers—writers who do not write. I wrote this whole book with a parent on each shoulder. I feel called to say to all nonwriting writers: *Writing is not for the timid type of person. You are brave enough!*

I am willing to ford the self-loathing, the despair, the difficulty. I am willing to do the hard work—the lazy hours, the writing hours, the sweating-hard hours, the fear hours, the intensity of it—because my parents, and so many of my students and their parents, write-but-don't.

If you asked them, my parents would say they are writers.

They adore writers. Their homes are filled with books. They think writing and writers are just as important, probably more, than praying and priests.

My parents will tell you they think writers are brilliant and fabulous.

My parents, raised in the Midwest during the Depression, don't think they themselves, or anyone they could know (or raise) could be brilliant and fabulous. My parents, like so many of my students and friends, hold writers in the highest esteem, and secretly want to call themselves writers, and sometimes do ... but they don't write. My parents don't feel, I think, that they could be writers. They are too scared of being judged. Their pride makes them brittle.

My dad is a coal miner's son. My mom is a blacksmith's daughter.

These people don't sit around saying, "I'm a writer." It would be like saying, "I'm God."

By becoming a writer, choosing this hard, thrilling, countercultural path, I am—I really believe this—saving and setting free my parents.

Not all of us can become writers.

Some of us raise writers. Some of us marry them. Some of us teach writers. Some of us decide not to become writers.

It is the ones in the goofy gap of fear I'm worried about. The nonwriting writers. The fear-bound.

My parents do everything writers do—worry, make notes, read a lot, fall in love with words, write to writers, watch shows about writers, memorize Mark Twain passages, recite poems from memory. My parents both cut out book reviews from the newspaper that they think their children should read, talk about ideas for books, give other people ideas for their books, learn new words well into their seventies, hold strong opinions on a wide range of complex ideas, manage anxiety, and worry about their next book. My parents look up words they don't know. They have library cards. They know books are sacred.

The only thing my parents don't do is write.

It was hard for me to realize all of this about my parents. I wanted them to be writers. They wanted themselves to be writers. We all sort of pretended they were writers, and they are, in so many ways. So close.

What keeps me going through the humiliation of writing weak stuff, the horrors of learning how to read my work in public, the long, hard days of feeling lazy, selfish, and strange?

I saw the price my parents paid—unhappiness—for not being brave enough to follow their writing dream, to make it real. I devoted myself, early on, to writing. Really writing. Just doing it, no matter how awkward and unfit I felt.

So, every single morning I am on the planet, I grit my teeth and do this hard, embarrassing, abject, thrilling thing—writing—because I want, in part, to count; I want my parents to live through me.

I want to be the honest, *right* version of what they had in mind. They are the draft; I am the next draft. And as drafts always go, always, I might be making it worse before I make it better, but one thing is for sure: My parents wanted to be and are (sort of, vaguely) writers, desperately and hugely; I sit down, each day, just about, except on the days I don't. And I write.

And I call myself a Writer.

Because I write words down.

I know how hard that is to do. Putting the actual words down on actual paper is the hardest thing.

Cleaning a toilet, paying bills, complaining, lashing out, going off medication, picking a fight, solving a friend's psychodrama—all those things are easy.

Writing is hard. It takes so much willingness to be bad at something. It's not fun to suck. And, if you are to write, suck you must.

I have the courage to write because I saw how intense and warping the fear of writing is.

My parents were both extraordinarily damaged by locking up all that writer-energy, by not allowing it to come out and find its form. My parents are dream-deferred poster children.

In my kid-mind logic, I believed I could save them pain and embarrassment if I became a writer. Now I know that I became a writer because if I learned one thing in my childhood, it was this: *The only thing harder and scarier and more white-knuckle difficult to sustain than an active, productive writing life is a not-writing life when you really, really dream and want to be a writer.*

For most people, the rents have to be dealt with, on some level, in relation to your writing life. I can't personally imagine Saul Bellow had lots of rents issues. Gertrude Stein? Danielle Steel? *Who* are *their* rents? I cannot imagine, and that is the point.

Loving your parents is good.

Setting them free—no matter what your age—is your next step. Separate your parents' relationship to your writing from your own.

Trust me: You *need* the space.

Add new writing parents. I have photographs of my favorite writers hanging in my writing space. Read the biographies and interviews of famous writers (see the appendix for specific sources) and choose a writing mother and a writing father.

If you like the way this is redirecting your confident writing energy, go ahead and expand your family. Choose a writing aunt, add a few writerly nephews, some neighbors, a whole little town of people who actually do write who are related to you. Goofy as it is, making a collage with these people's faces (photocopy writer photos at the library) and sticking up inspiring quotes by them really helps the rents take up less space and gives your writing parents the space they deserve. It's hard to really establish that writing groove—daily practice—if you have your real parents still calling the shots. (Even, or especially if, they were great parents!) Claim your new writing parents. An ancient Chinese sage can be your distant great-great-grandfather, Virginia Woolf can be your aunt, Pablo Neruda can be your great-uncle! Know their faces and their words, and they *will* guide you. Claim your ancestors.

This really works!

Chapter 10

Anxiety

WRITERS ARE PEOPLE WHO ARE COMFORTABLE WITH INTENSE contradictions. They are the people who live with a high degree of anxiety. Becoming a writer means learning how to write, every day, without missing a day. In order to do this, writers have to gently embrace ambivalence, anxiety, not-sure-ness.

While unpleasant, this practice of writing while in a state of anxiety is key to making a writing life. It's way more important than learning plot or prosody or publication tips.

Many of the productive writers I know believe they are simultaneously shit and undiscovered geniuses. Brilliant shit. This belief is in itself anxiety-producing.

Not knowing if you suck or are the next Anne Tyler/ Stephen King/Albert Camus is simply very frustrating and irritating. It's a weird way to live.

It's how we live.

Writers are people who tolerate a high level of anxiety. We have a talent for holding up well under tension.

Maybe even thriving on it.

Maybe one reason a lot of writers come from chaotic households is that we are the kind of people who can survive chaos. Some writers don't come from chaotic families. But they are also able to withstand intense sustained anxiety. In other words, you don't need a screwed-up childhood in order to write (as some of my students from wonderful, loving homes worry). You do need to increase your fluency in the inner workings of your personality.

If you want to write or if you are a writer, you maintain, in part, a glorious sense of self. You live inside a soul that desires to create. Just like God, you create! This is thrilling and intoxicating and hugely gratifying.

Naturally, you have been told, many times, you are not actually God, get over yourself. So you aren't sure. That's the root of anxiety. Are you a fool? Should you really be taking four hours away from your family on the weekends in order to do this selfish writing thing? What is the point of all this writing? Why do it at all? Do you suck horribly? Can you write? You will never know the answers. Every single writer I know has some doubt or enormous paralyzing doubt. How we manage this doubt—which is just part of the deal for writers, it comes with the job—is the subject of this chapter.

Most people can write, using the burst of excitement that comes from getting in touch with that desire—I'm going to write! They ride that wave, into shore, and, depending on how it felt, they go back out for more, or, they just *think* about writing, that good feeling. Underneath all the writing pleasure is a solid substructure that I will call anxiety. It never goes away.

And, in fact, you don't want it to. You need anxiety. Think of anxiety as cops. They can be irritating, but remember, laws make man free. We may not adore law enforcement (or we might), but we need to have the ability to call someone if our car is stolen or our house is broken into. In your writing life, you are going to have fierce forces arresting your best ideas.

Every time you write. It's part of the deal.

Any one can start writing. To *keep* on creating and to grow as a writer, you also believe you suck. You question each thing you write. There are good ways to do this, and less good ways; I'll explain in a moment. I know writing students who really do seem to believe they are great, they love writing, they write a lot, they seem blandly cheerful, they don't revise. They spew out words. They have no doubt, they reveal no anxiety. I think that is great—there aren't any police in their town, roughing up the wrong man, citing little old ladies for driving too slowly. But, my students who are doing really fine work, really committing themselves to writing honestly, deeply, and truly—they have anxiety. They doubt themselves all the time. Writing stuff that is going to affect other people intensely is walking a fine line between anxiety and pleasure—it's a vibe you ride.

Doubt is a dance, and you have to learn a few steps so that the doubt-dance becomes *useful* to your process and not debilitating. And, hear this: You are going to go overboard with doubt, again and again. You are going to fall on the floor. Each time you do, get up, brush yourself off, and say: This is part of the deal. This is *part* of writing. An essential part.

Try looking at doubt and anxiety in a whole new way. Being unsure is one of the things that helps you steer in revision. If you just pour forth and leave everything you write just as it came out, it probably won't be your best work. Learning how to get underneath or above or beside judgment when you are writing, and then to call in the exact right judicial authority when it's time to expand or contract your piece of writing—this is an art!

Make doubt your ally. Tell your anxiety you appreciate him. Say to these voices: Thanks for showing up, for keeping me honest, I'm glad I have you in my town. However, no crime is being committed here, and I need you to go down to the diner, eat some hash and eggs, and I'll phone if and when I need you. Okay?

The first ninety times you tell them this, they aren't going to believe a word you say. These are *law enforcement officials*. You have been crying *help* for a long time. You will have to convince them, through repetition and tenacity, that you are quite serious, quite capable of writing without them. Or with them very nearby. And like a young parent, they are going to hear your screams while you are working, mistake play for pain, and come rushing in at all the wrong moments, loaded for bear. You can laugh. You can remember: This is what a writing life looks like. This is the main part of it you can count on. Anxiety. Look—here it comes. It's part of the deal.

Anxiety is part of the force that makes us create. It is a force that can be used for good, once it is understood. When you work on a piece of writing, when you want to finish it, become happy with it, you destroy it. You might not have thought of it this way, but when you change your piece (and I believe this is why so many writers hesitate to revise) you do kill it, its baby incarnation. This is not pleasant! Finishing means changing. Change requires something to die. Yikes! Revising means reshaping, undoing, pushing deeper. Creating means modifying and modifying means destroying something. And here is the clincher: You never know if you are making it better or worse. Writing is like living in the dark. You don't know. You have hope. You have all your other senses, but you have to trust this scary force—anxiety mixed with pleasure. It's a very weird way to live.

[80]

Writers are people walking around with both of these selves—God self and nervous self. It's not a particularly comfortable mode of life. Writers are the people who are able to survive this constant worrying—these loops of anxious chatter—and even thrive in it. When you are slaying demons on a daily basis (yes, you will have to do this every time you write, every time!) you get a kind of wizened, cocky, and fabulous look about you.

Study anxiety.

The best way to manage anxiety is to shine a little light on it. Resisting it makes it worse. Light makes it vanish (if only temporarily). What is light in this case? Putting words down on paper. If you continue on as though nothing is really wrong, the cops will, eventually, go back down to the diner or to another neighborhood. It's the work that makes demons vanish. Thinking about the work feeds them, and they love that—they become huge and fanged and monstrous: They feed on raw thoughts! Work terrifies them—you don't need demons if you are working.

Rollo May, in *The Meaning of Anxiety*, writes that anxiety is a basic response. When we think our *personality* is under attack, that our core essence is vulnerable, we respond with anxiety. When we meet attack with fear, we protect the inner citadel of ourself. When we respond with anxiety, the invasion is already underway. It's too late for fear—we feel overwhelmed and are subject to fear's corollaries, panic, and frantic behavior.

How to write, then? Well, we have to start worrying earlier in the process. This sounds screwy, I know. Bear with me.

Fear is the self's armor against anxiety. We want to stay with fear a little bit more. Delay the armoring process. Fear is useful. Anxiety is numbing. It's a drug. Drugs keep us from our creations.

What you want to do is ask yourself: What are you afraid of?

Work on spending more time with fear, delaying, if only for a micromoment, anxiety, fear's ugly cloak.

ON YOUR PAGE: *Exercise 20*

Get into a comfortable position, in your bed or on your sofa, or in a café where you like to write. Get out your notebook. Write at the top of a fresh page "Writing Fears." Number your list from one to twenty-five. You're going to have to write fast—fears are like cockroaches, they scatter when you turn the light on and imbed themselves deeper in … you have to move fast to catch them. Three minutes—go. List every fear—and keep your pencil moving. You have to put something down for all twenty-five items, make up stuff if you are stuck, write other people's fears, just get this done in three minutes. (You can do almost anything for three minutes.) Don't worry if what you are writing is stupid and makes no sense. Is that your first fear? "I'm stupid, make no sense." Pay attention—just as you are reading this, your fears are rising up—see 'em?

Here's my list of writing fears from today:

1. *I suck.*
2. *This is a waste of time.*
3. *My grammar is not that great.*
4. *I haven't read enough books.*
5. *I can't remember what I read.*
6. *I'm writing the same book over and over.*
7. *I'm just not smart enough to be a writer.*
8. *I nap too often.*

9. *I'm ignoring my children and husband.*
10. *People are dying.*
11. *I'm selfish.*
12. *I'm lazy.*
13. *It's still a waste of time.*
14. *I really hate writing.*
15. *I don't want to really be a writer that much.*
16. *It's way too much work, and I have a brain injury.*
17. *I should use this time for exercising.*
18. *Everything has been said.*
19. *I can't even finish this list!*
20. *My writing is ugly and disorganized.*
21. *I don't even know where all my drafts are on my computer.*
22. *I should be teaching and making money—this is an expensive hobby.*
23. *Writing is self-indulgent.*
24. *I have nothing to say.*
25. *Thank god this list is done, what is the point, of this, of writing?*

This exercise is hard to do. I felt my throat closing up while I was doing it. When I got to number twenty-one, I felt my stomach swirl. I hated it. I felt the exercise was stupid, and I felt like a failure for not being able to do it well, easily. It was really hard! To write for three minutes, to think of twenty-five things. ... I kept wondering, *Why am I doing this?* And I kept thinking, *Wow, I'm really, really bad at this.*

Tips for Success
If you have only done the exercise in your head—if you are one of those people who buys lots of writing and self-help books and then does all the exercises in your head, you at this point must get over

yourself, sit down, and physically actually write down the twenty-five things in three minutes.

Okay.

Now, pay attention to how you felt. Those feelings—frustration in your heart, itching in your wrists, grouchiness in your brain—whatever you felt, those are your cops. It's important that you recognize fear and its poorly paid henchmen. This is them. They come by often, don't they. So often, you are entirely used to them!

The truth is this: The henchmen are part of the deal. Anxiety will show up. You do not have to employ it, though. You can, with practice (remember, ninety days, in a row, of practice! So much!) send these dudes packing. Tell them to come back when you are done.

ON YOUR PAGE: *Exercise 21*

Take the first item on your list from above: #1: "I suck." Pretend you have been arrested, fined, taken down to the station for "sucking." You have written bad writing. What's the punishment? There actual-ly—surprise—isn't one, is there? The cops—are sputtering, the whole thing seems ridiculous! What did you do? Wrote poorly? Good! You wrote! Most people don't even do that.

Divide a sheet of paper into two columns. On the left side, the cops get to talk—they explain all the ways in which you suck, they read your lack of rights to you, they detail the accusations. Let them rip. On you.

On your side of the sheet, your defense. In detail. Why is it okay for you to suck? Well, first of all, it isn't a crime. It's healthy for peo-ple to spend more time writing, less time stressing and dreaming and not-doing writing. You are getting to know yourself and paying attention to the world. It isn't hurting anyone, and it probably, ulti-mately, is helping people. You are even helping yourself by taking action instead of walking around, in your head all the time. That's the real crime! Having a dream, and not ever acting on it ... if you can't defend yourself, hire a lawyer. Write down your defense. Your rationale. Teach the judge. You can do it; explain #1.

Your next steps are obvious—you do the same for all twenty-five. Whenever you get swamped or stuck, or if a few days have gone by and you notice you have not written anything down, do one of these. Repeat as needed. You can't do it in your head.

This is real.

This is court.

This is anxiety. This is how you deal with it.

Write down what you notice.

Chapter 11

Being Away From the Work

THE OTHER TITLE FOR THIS PIECE IS: "WAKE UP WRITING."

There is a famous quote: If you take one day off writing, your muse will take the next three.

The more time you take off writing, the more difficult it is to get absorbed into that state of total concentration—focus—some call it flow.

If you haven't been writing for years or months, it will take you ten days of steady writing, horrible yucky not-good days, in order to get (back in) the habit.

With that evil little truism in mind, how long does it take to write a book?

I know a lot of writers. Some of them write a book a year. Some of these books are terrible, hastily conceived, sloppily executed books (and I'd be happy enough, I suppose, to write them). Others are writing series in genres. They write a book a year about their detective or their sleuth. The books are good. And they sell.

Then, there are writers I don't know at all, but they also write a book a year, and professors everywhere designate these as the best books in the world, and they are. Writers like Iris Murdoch and Doris Lessing. A book a year, or so, and their books are rich and thick and deeply layered and full of brilliant observations and dense philosophies and vibrant sensory scenes.

Most writers I know don't write a book a year (A brilliant page a day? Ten sucky pages a day for a month, then eleven months to revise?). They don't write anything close to it. Most writers I know write a book every five years. And some of these efforts are published.

The secret to writing a book: Don't miss a day.

What happens when you miss a day?

This week, I missed four days of writing from Thursday to yesterday, which was Sunday. Sunday afternoon, I hid from my husband and children. I locked myself in the bathroom. I drew a bath, only I sat on the floor, not in the bathtub, with my ratty red journal and a blue ink pen, and I wrote down words. I had to write. I had to write something. I listed funny things the boys had said this last week.

They weren't very funny when I wrote them down. Nothing like they were in real life. But I wrote two pages in my journal—just scratched down stuff. The whole time I was wondering why I was writing this down. I made little lists. I couldn't even write sentences. I was stiff. I was out of shape.

I used to flip out when I couldn't write during the three days I spent waiting for my muse to return.

This is such an uncomfortable, horrible feeling, I try to avoid missing days. The not-writing days aren't worth it! It's too hard to get back into it. This is why athletes cross-train off season. This is why people who are successful with weight management stay below a certain weight. It just isn't worth it. Getting back into shape is just too hard. It is easier to keep doing it, tiny little writing periods, day after day.

Without missing a day.

And, if you do miss a day, or two, or seven, or a few years, realize this one key thing: You will have a period of horrible writing days where you question everything about why you are doing it. The writing will stink. You will hate doing it. Then you will get the magic back, but only by going through the gross horrible woods of despair. The failure rate is high.

I asked my friend Nancy who is eighty and a runner how she keeps doing it. "You never want to get into the state of mind where you are deciding if you are going to go on your run or not. Get out the door." That was her whole secret!

I show up every day (it has taken me years of practice, but I am pretty good now) in my writing room because I want to demonstrate to myself that I am capable of commitment, of practice.

The less I think about it, the less I angst about it.

This morning, for example, I got out of bed and started writing. Most mornings are like that.

It took me a long, long time to develop this practice, with hundreds of false starts and failures and many pages of writing that is just that—writing.

But it's so worth it!

I wanted to be a writer. And, I feel like I am. You can do this. Anyone can. You just have to wake up, writing.

I have decided that I am a five-year book writer. All those days I spend not writing and wrestling myself back into the groove? That's all part of my writing life. I take a long time. My projects take me a long, long time.

I know something is brewing when I am not writing, and I also know my mind simply isn't brewing all week long, day and night. Cooks don't cook around the clock. Baseball players sometimes go to the mall or watch television. Parties and friends and volunteering at the rest home, all that is part of my week and should be.

Writing for me is a slow, slow process. I only get a little bit done each week. Am I using my time wisely? Not always. I think I might do better when I'm not keeping track. When I am not knowing, not noticing, not counting pages, hours, words, publication credits.

Being away from the work gives me good perspective. As long as I have done the work that day, the not-working time is fulfilling and useful and important and pleasurable. But if I haven't written, being away from the work feels draining or worse.

I try to set my life up between two long straight true rails. The rail of writing practice on one side. The rail of spiritual _____ (there isn't really a word for it—but the closest I can get would be growth or awareness or practice or play—but none of those are the right words) on the other side. I generally try to choose thoughts and actions that fit inside the tracks of writing practice and _____.

I find that I gather momentum when I stay in the tracks. I find myself being kinder to myself when I run off the track. Many train wrecks per day are not unusual. I'm getting so much better at reloading myself, putting myself back on track. When I fling myself outside my groove, I'm flinging myself closer to the rails, so the walk back isn't so grueling.

This morning, I awoke with writing momentum. I wrote down a few words—223 (I just counted them) to be exact—in my red journal. I went to sleep. I didn't think a lot more about it. Then, I *found* myself at the computer. I wafted to it, no pressure, no agenda, just *there*.

That, for me, is the most successful, the most on track, the happiest I can be. This is a very rare writing day, and it's the best kind. No doubts, no questioning. I feel like a smart cute monk, in prayer, and making a fine soup. It's just what I do.

More normal is this kind of day: I go to bed at 8:30 P.M. I set the alarm for 5 A.M. I will get up right then and get to work on the novel, and also stop drinking and lose five pounds.

When the alarm beeps on this kind of (typical, frequent, normal writer day), I flick it right off. Back to sleep. Don't think about writing, or not writing, and then at 7:30 A.M., I get up and go straight to the computer. (I want to replicate this state of affairs on a daily basis—but the point of this chapter is *you can't*.)

The lazy down days are part of the up days.

Any day you are writing anything at all, even one sentence, is a cause for celebration. It's that hard, what we are trying to do. Keep that in mind, and also the equally true thing—if I can do this, you can.

Ride your tracks gently, gently.

When I take three days off writing, it takes me six to get my rhythm back. I know that now (after fifteen years of practice), and I wade through the bad days, knowing the good days *will* come back.

If I just stay with it.

The other thing we know about the muse: She visits writers who are at their desks, writing.

When you are off track, away from the work, what can you notice about how you get back on? Do you need some more tools, a jack, a wheel fixer, a crowbar? What would help you? You need more track maintenance dollars in your budget, so you don't fall off so often.

Can you show up without thinking about it? No programs, no plans? No rituals, no excess? Just show up, and write? Can you stop thinking about writing and being famous and sucking so badly, and simply move your pencil across the page—less drama, more work?

One way to think about these questions purposefully is to write out answers to them. Some people use their nondominant hand, and find the answers that come up quite surprising. Try it. Interview yourself with your dominant hand, writing out the questions above, or any others this chapter poses. Answer with your other hand. You will have to write slowly. That's good.

Get a timer. Lay out, on a nice flat surface, two blank sheets of paper and a good pen or sharp pencil. Set the timer for ten minutes. Do anything but write for ten minutes. You are not allowed to write or even think about writing. Bother other students in your class, harangue your kids, or fold laundry, take a walk, dust, do dishes, call a friend. Pay bills. Or, sit and space out, if you are the kind of person capable of that sort of free-floating mind.

When the timer rings, you have to *run, not walk* to the desk, reset the timer for another ten minutes, and in these ten minutes fill those two pages, hand not stopping. If you don't know how to start, start by listing all the teachers you can remember, from the first to the most recent, and write fast, be messy. If a teacher grabs you and wants to be written about more, let her in. Or, begin by describing a time when you were eleven years old and in someone else's house or car. You have to be able to give yourself assignments that you haven't hashed over, and you have to be willing to follow your own trail. When doubt and fear step in to stop you (they will, you count on that, you know that's going to happen) you say (loudly), "Leave me alone! I have to fill these pages in ten minutes; do you want me to fail?"

This act—a timed assignment—will silence your internal critics. They want you to do well.

ON YOUR PAGE: *Exercise 24*

This is a trick you can use to wake up writing every day. I learned it from Lynda Barry, my teacher. Get twenty index cards. In block capitals, write down the words below (of course you can use any concrete nouns that have lots of meaning for you, or are drawn from your journals and writings). You can draw from this deck to do your daily ten minute timed writings—in the parking lot while your kid finishes soccer practice, when you wake up, when you can't sleep. Use the word to start your writing. Just keep your ever-growing deck in a little pouch, with your journal, or in your purse or wallet. Keep your cards in a baggie, and write at lunch for ten minutes. It's really important that you don't go over or under ten minutes.

Here are my twenty no-fail writing cards:

DOGS KITCHENS BRAS

BARS CHILDREN

TEACHERS CARS SHOES

BLUE SWIMMING POOLS

PREGNANT FATHERS

UNCLES THE DARK CANDY

FIRE BOOKS 5TH GRADE

SPIDERS DRUGS

Chapter 12
Reversing the Message

ONE DAY ANN WENT TO MEET HER NEW THERAPIST. ANN HAD never done therapy before. But her mom, whom she'd cared for for ten years (really her whole life, if you want to know—she was that kind of a mom, sweet, but very, very high maintenance), had just died, and Ann felt ready to drop some habits that weren't working.

Elisabeth, the therapist, was Italian, and she had a beautiful piazza of an office where she saw her clients in Black Mountain. It was Ann's first visit.

Elisabeth didn't talk at all.

Ann hated it. "Why am I paying to ramble on?" Ann said to me that night on the phone. "I told her to give me homework. I am a homework person. I need *assignments*."

I used to be exactly like this, too. But I just listened, very mouse-like, very good friend, as Ann hailed forth.

"So Elisabeth says she doesn't really give assignments. She doesn't believe in homework. But I made her give me home-work. So, I have homework!" Ann sounded proud.

"What is it?" I said. "What's the homework?" I imagined Ann bossing her therapist, making her therapy into a little class where she could get an A. Ann's a teacher. Isn't it funny how we get hidebound by our jobs? They become the only way we experience the world.

"I'm going to do it. Then I'll call you back. Okay? Okay!"

I love when people start therapy.

They remind me of my swimmers when I taught swimming as a girl in Florida. The water looks so good. It's another thing altogether to get in.

Ann called me back a few hours later. I was watching *The West Wing*, my favorite show of the moment. In this episode, Josh was in therapy. He hated it at first. Then, he started to notice some of his own bullshit. That made him happy, embarrassed, and more able to be humorous and easy with himself.

"Is this a bad time?" she said. "I just thought of something. This is a terrible therapist. I have the proof now."

"No, no," I said. "This is a great time. What's up?" Josh was busy with the president. I listened closely to Ann.

"Well, the homework was terrible! Cruel! Who would do such a thing," Ann proceeded to explain. Her homework was to write a letter to her least favorite body part, the part she really hated the most.

I breathed in. Then I breathed out. I imagined the Italian new-agey Elisabeth, on her mountain, in her terracotta and sage-scented world. "Ann," I said. "I think you wrote the assignment down wrong. Really, really wrong."

And she had.

The next week she learned Elisabeth had really said, of course, "Write a letter to the body part you love the most. The one you need to thank. The part you enjoy, but you never tell it."

Ann had reversed the message.

You need to watch yourself very closely as you learn to write. Your best intentions will be met with the wiliest kinds of resistance. Learning how to write better, deeper, longer, truer is a delicate balancing act. You want to learn to write, sure. But you also don't want to be told what to do, how to do it, to do things differently.

To actually be a writer, you have to be willing to be a different kind of person—maybe only slightly so, but still different from how you are right now. We say we want to be writers, but so much of us wants to also keep things just like they are right now! Wishing to write, and not actually doing it—we already know how to do that! We have had a lot of practice. It's not particularly pleasant, but it's known, and therefore easier.

Pay attention to how you learn, how you change, how growth happens for you. Are you pretending to learn more than you really are? Are you pushing the learning, or flailing, faking that it's way harder than it really is?

Learning is gentle, and it's thrilling, and it's sometimes a little nerve-racking. You leave what you know and trust, and go towards something new and different. Expect this to be messy, uncomfortable, and nonlinear.

Here's an activity for you to try. It's very touchy-feely, very tofu, very new agey, really it is. Do you resist that kind of activity?

Interesting.

Me, I'm a greedy little sucker. I am so eager to improve as a writer, I try everything. I'm a fabulously great slut (which is really a kind of information gathering process, no?) when it comes to the writing world—I try everything that threatens to teach me something new.

How about you?

Are you willing to try?

Read the messages on the next page to yourself. After you read one, listen. Listen softly, gently. What does your gut hear when you say the words? Your throat? The back of your mind? Your spine?

Are there ways you notice you might be reversing the message?

When I read "You can write," in any number of the writing books I collected when I was in college, I *know* I was always reversing that message. Somehow between my eyeball and my brain, I got it twisted up and told myself, "You can't write. Everyone else can. This book is not for you. Why are you even reading it?"

My resistance took many forms (I am a very creative person): This book is too high brow. This book is too low brow. This book is too crystals and incense. This book is not intuitive enough. This book is for beginners. This book is for advanced, experienced writers.

And none of those were me.

Except they were all me.

Why did Ann want homework from her brand-new therapist anyway? Well, she was terrified to jump in the water—who isn't? We are all afraid to start something as productive, deep, intense, and meaningful as swimming, dieting, therapy, or God forbid, a writing life. Homework can protect us from growth.

We might not like this old body (pool, heart, blank page, waistline, etc.), but dammit, it's ours, we know it. The known is safer. The unknown—change—is supposed to be terror-inducing.

How can you get more comfortable in your skin? With your writing self?

Simple. Listen and practice. What messages are you sending to your writing self?

Practice paying attention.

Practice listening to yourself.

Are you reversing the positive messages? Do you clutter the messages with a bunch of qualifiers (oh, but, not, no not really, sort of, well sometimes, oh I don't know, this is stupid!, not really, oh ...)? What do you hear?

You are a writer.

You are perfect, just as you are.

You can write a novel by the end of next year.

You can write a novel in six weeks.

You have the power to change your life and write as much as you want.

Your fear isn't working for you anymore.

You are a fabulous succulent writer.

You are good.

You are okay: sometimes great, sometimes not.

There is no need to do more than listen. If you did listen, and nothing happened, try it again. If you aren't used to noticing your own mind, all its dark little cupboards and rusty counters, you might have to practice this a bit more. Try distracting yourself—send yourself messages while you are brushing your teeth, for example. See if you can hear, deep, deep inside, under the carpets of your soul, little voices saying, *No.*

Shedding light, the great flashlight of courage and its bulb, intuition, on these voices is the way to let them know their services aren't particularly required anymore.

Thank them, and dismiss them.

(Or, if you were raised in this kind of home say, "Screw you and screw off. I'm trying to learn something here.")

ON YOUR PAGE: *Exercise 25*

You don't need homework. Homework is a distraction that keeps us from doing our real work, our real learning. Homework is the water wings of therapy and of writing instruction. Homework and exercises can keep you from learning how to swim by keeping you afloat, falsely. It's the illusion of doing great things, covering much territory. But you can never go really deep with big orange air-puffed floaties on your arms!

Jump in. With force and enthusiasm.

If you aren't ready, if the water is too cold, if you can't get naked yet, that is fine. Practice standing on shore, listening.

Listen. Learn. Your resistance is your guide. Don't reverse the message. This week, write without prompts, without exercise. Go deeper than you have before. Go on your own. You can do it.

Part 2

Turning Pages:
How to Maintain Your
Commitment to Writing

Chapter 13
Blank and Cranky

MY MIND WAS BLANK AND BEING CRANKY. A FULL, bristling, itching blank. This is a terrible combination. It was a Monday night. I had signed up for Monday night yoga, but I didn't want to go.

I decided once again that I didn't really like the yoga teacher and my time would be better spent doing anything but horrible, boring yoga, which was just a stupid craze for middle-class people with too much time on their hands anyway.

So, I drove right on past The Yoga Loft, and I drove cranky Heather right back home.

I walked in my house feeling numb and dumb, and looked for something on television to watch, thought I'd pay bills.

I couldn't find anything to watch. I looked at all the receipts and felt bad for buying so much stuff, and not keeping track.

The qualities that make me an artist are the ability to obsess on minutiae and the ability to feel intensely.

These qualities also make me prone to being swamped by a mood and getting sidetracked by obsessive worrying.

This number we do in our heads, well, we like it when it's helping us write our novels.

But we don't like our artist-mind when it is fixated on real life and little problems. When an artist has a mood, it's always a Big Deal. This is how the work gets done. This is also how the work doesn't get done.

Think how productive you'd be if you could redirect the mood, fill the cranky blanks with poetry!

What many people do when they are swamped by a bad mood is to call in the disciplinarian and put themselves on a program.

Terrible idea.

A bad mood *in writers* responds best to invitation and napping. Those two things.

A bad mood is like an infant. You can't discipline an infant. You have to just give in and cuddle it, even if it isn't the sweetest cutest thing at that moment. Especially if it isn't the sweetest cutest thing.

The secret to life is this: invitation.

Discipline will not work.

The secret to getting more work done is a little bit tricky, because it feels completely counterintuitive. If you want to pay your bills or get caught up on six months of unbalanced checkbook or start a new writing routine or do yoga, for that matter, the first thing you must do when the inevitable cranky horror mood strikes is nap.

Nap.

Yup, nap.

I'm not kidding.

That Monday night, when I couldn't get out of the bad mood or into a downward dog, I got in bed, at 7:30 P.M. and I went to sleep. I woke up writing in the morning. Not in a great mood, but at least working.

On our morning run, my friend Betsy told me that she wanted very badly to get a lot of writing done this week, and also get caught up with work because she was sick and in bed all day yesterday and didn't get anything done. "I am so behind!" she hollered as we rounded the corner by the football fields.

Betsy was coughing as we ran across the sand flats. I said, "Betsy, go home, right now. Stop running! This is crazy."

"I can't," she said. "I can't stay in bed another day."

Oh dear.

I knew Betsy was going to have a horrible writing session, and write all kinds of wrong addresses down on her bill-paying envelopes, and probably lose her keys, too.

Here is the secret to life, the secret to writing, and to productivity. (Be forewarned: People are not going to like it that you know the secret to life. So prepare for this. Most of the time, people who claim they have secrets to life are arrested, killed, ostracized, or all three.) Here's the secret: When you are cranky, down on yourself, behind, overwhelmed, blue, swamped; when you are saying, *I need to write! I don't have time! I have to write, I'm behind*; when you are sick or getting sick or recently sick, you must nap.

I know this sounds: (a) stupid, and (b) impossible.

I know you don't want to nap; you want to get caught up, and you have to or life will fall apart.

That plan never, ever works. Abandon it.

All these sick, stressed-out, busy, cranky, behind people come to work, come to the desk, force themselves on task, and get all the rest of us sick and cranky and overwhelmed and depressed.

Stop the madness.

You need to wallow. When your kid is loudly singing, "The song that never ends, some people started it and blah blah blah it goes on and on my friends! It's the song that never ends!"

you must pull the car over. Breathe in all that kid-singing horror, lay your head down gently on the wheel, and say, as you drift off for a baby-nap, "Sing louder."

To get rid of the thing you don't want, you can't reject it. You have to go into it further. This makes no sense, I know, but it really, really works.

The way to get out of a nonproductive mood is to stay in it as long as possible. This is hard to do.

This full frontal wallowing makes the mood a bit confused. Confusion is good—confusion at least gets the energy moving around.

Take the night off. Do nothing. (Nap or wallow—these are your only two choices. That's what you are going to be doing anyway, perhaps with the veneer of activity, but your work won't be good work. Give it up. Get over yourself.)

Skip class. Lie about your whereabouts.

Artists are vagabond outlaws—we lie, we hide out, we don't cooperate. We must do this more.

Confuse the bad mood by taking to your bed with a glass of wine; trashy, easy-to-read, juicy books; pens; and paper. And do nothing.

These are your toys. You can throw them on the floor.

Wallow!

And then, sleep.

You aren't going to have a great writing day if you whip yourself into it, like Betsy was trying to do. Nor are you going to have a good writing day if you drive around doing errands and paying bills and thinking about how far behind in your writing you've gotten, how horrible you are.

There is only one solution, and it is this: Nap.

Nap and nestle right on into that bad mood, chew on it. Let it become full blown gnarly insomnia if it wants. Tell it: I am staying up. I will never, ever sleep again.

If you pay attention to the kid screaming at you, total attention, he will feel "seen" and get bored by your attention and will leave you alone. If you withhold, though, he'll keep needing, needing, needing.

If you give it your undivided attention—no holding back— your bad mood will get bored and go away.

With a diet of steady napping and days off, what happens is magical. And strange. After a few months of doing this, you are going to find yourself having fewer ugly moods.

I know this sounds crazy.

And, I know it is very hard to set your life up so that you are able to let so many down, taking to your room whenever you are cranky.

But listen—when you are getting sick, you aren't getting anything done. When you are super cranky, you are going through the motions, but you're screwing up so much, it's hardly worth it!

In this case, the wallowing way is the fastest way to get through a bad mood. It's shorter and more efficient in the long run. One day off, completely off—call it a mental health vacation day—is better for your whole life's productivity than three days done grumpily.

Enjoy your day off! Don't feel all guilty and strange! You deserve to lay in bed feeling semi-okay, recharging. You don't have to just lie in bed when you are sick and puking. If you lie in bed sometimes *before* you get to the puking flu stage, you will get sick less often. And people will like you more.

Think of your artist self as going through a stage. We all go through them. Look down the road three months. You can. I know, you are already seizing up, *This is the only year I have to write! I don't have three months! My life isn't like yours.*

Yes, it is. You can lie in bed sick. You take off when you are too ill, right? Start taking off when you are healthy. You really can do this.

You have the same amount of minutes in a day as every one else. And you have sick days, or at least sick hours, too.

And you aren't getting that writing down anyway, or you wouldn't be reading this book. You have to be able to waste time. To spend it, luxuriously, in order to write. You must learn this skill.

ON YOUR PAGE: *Exercise 26*

So try it. Practice with a pretend bad mood.

Get used to the motion: Conjure crankiness and cave in. Conjure and cave in. Go get in your bed—right now, in the middle of the day. Cancel your plans. Say you are under the weather. You have this as homework, okay?

Go nap. Get really comfy. Settle in. For a couple of hours. Do whatever you would do if you were extremely, violently, ill. Engage your emergency back-up people and systems, and take the time.

It's the secret to life.

ON YOUR PAGE: *Exercise 27*

When is obsessing useful to the artist, and how do we manage the little warring factions of obsessive energies? When you are trying to lose weight, you might keep a food journal. Hard to do, but it does let people around you know you are serious about being more conscious of food, its role in your life. Letting other people know what you are up to helps you stay honest. Keeping a journal or a log of any kind (even if no one sees it) is a way of publicizing your attempts. It makes your actions more real.

For one week, try keeping a mood log (this is hard, hard, hard to do, but it's *nothing* compared to writing a novel! Think of it as a micromovement).

Every time you think of it, check in.

A few times a day, more if you are into this kind of thing, jot down your mood. What's going on? Are you obsessing? Thinking the same thoughts over and over? Are you dreaming of how your life could be? Note it down.

Tips for Success

You want to cultivate a clear blank—a mind that is open, vulnerable, and plain. Empty, basically, of thought. This is a writing mind. When you are empty, you are able to focus.

The very act of noticing when you have a writing mind during the day will help you cultivate your writing life. You'll be able to recognize and expand those flashes of time conducive to working. You will notice that you are more loving, more creative, more thoughtful, whenever you are in this calm blank state. You are simply being in the present.

A thousand distractions come your way during a writing session. But you learn, by noticing what this state of mind is, to stretch it out, make it last longer. In order to write, you have to be able to fall back into this state of mind—completely relaxed and completely able to focus.

You'll move toward it with practice, because it feels so good.

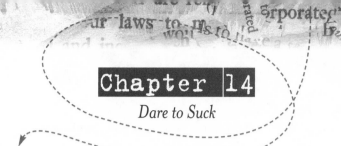

Chapter 14

Dare to Suck

YOU DON'T KNOW WHERE THE NEXT GREAT STORY IS COMING from. Is that not enough motivation for you to keep writing? You need to write your next piece. And your next one. You need to keep writing.

Can anyone become a great writer? Probably not. It takes an ability to focus, a heart that is tinged with wisdom, and a hunger. But I have taught classes where I have been amazed at every single person's writing, just flat on the floor amazed. I believe absolutely that writing can be taught—of course it can. And I believe anyone can learn writing technique. But, there's a catch. You have to be able to tolerate your own bad writing. If you are going to get better, you are going to have to suck.

In writing school, I wrote a lot.

I sucked. My first story was about a girl who meets a priest on a dock. It sucked so bad, that story. Why would a girl meet a priest on a dock? No reason. What would they say to each other? Nothing.

Then I started getting better.

All my friends were writers, too. They sucked, and they were in the process of getting better, as well. Jamie wrote his first story about digging a giant hole in the yard. Then he wrote his second story about his governess. It was really, really good.

When we weren't writing, we were draped in the famous local oyster bar, the Grand Finale. We were cute, cool, and

crazily happy with our great good fortune—we were The
Writers.

We liked punk music, and black eyeliner, and boys who
wrote lyrics. We liked bad movies and cigarettes and ceviche
and striped shirts, like Picasso's.

We were amazingly cool.

After about two years of this, humming along in a pack,
fueled by oysters and workshop and longnecks and great teachers, Derek arrived. He was from Australia, and he was white.
He had an English accent. Not an Australian accent. So he
seemed wrong.

It was spring semester. Few people start school in spring.

His first short story was a disastrous, typo-ridden, barely
grammatical thing. The prof handed it back to him. We were
secretly thrilled. We didn't need any competition. Publicly,
Derek was whipped. Derek. Poor Derek. He was so odd. He
had an odd wife, older than he was, with messy hair. She wrote
too. "Oh, a writing couple," we lamented, even though most
of us were in the same configuration. Derek was pale and
ruddy, mostly bald, and he talked in a loud voice. His white
thick cotton shirts were unbuttoned to midchest. His khaki
pants seemed to always be the same, tired pair. He wore sandals. He didn't go to Finale. He and his wife lived in a camper.
They were always together.

"That was a weird story," I said about Derek's story, in our
workshop postmortem at the bar. It was my favorite part of
class, the after-class.

No one else said anything.

Oh, Derek.

We didn't make fun of Derek behind his back. His story was

so terrible, his personality so *different*—even we could see it would have been cruel.

I figured Derek would drop out after the first semester. A writer that bad—you would quit, right?

We often forgot to invite Derek and his wife to our parties.

One day in the hall we were all milling around waiting for class to start.

"Hello," Derek said, loudly and cautiously. "Your bikini girls piece was the tops, really the tops, I thought, didn't I?" He looked at his spouse, and she nodded tensely.

I said, cautiously, trying to be very friendly, "What are you working on?"

"I don't know, Heather. I don't rightly know, right off. Let me review for myself some of what's been knocking around in my head." Derek went into a long, long story about his works in progress. There were many. He'd written a screenplay. He and his wife were co-authoring a novel together. He had ideas for six novels. He said, "It seems like such a lot!" There were other stories and all kinds of ideas.

I graduated, got a job, didn't think about Derek. I wrote stories about girls who live in bikinis and the people who love them. I felt superior and lonely, and I never, ever once thought about Derek. Ever.

I subscribe to a lot of literary magazines. *Glimmer Train*, *The Missouri Review*, *The New Yorker*, of course, and *Tin House*, *The Chattahoochee Review*, *New Virginia Review*, *Beloit Fiction Journal*, *The Paris Review*. I love reading stories and poems and interviews by up-and-coming authors.

One day I was sitting by the pool in my apartment complex, three years after plucking my Ph.D. handily from Florida State

University, a smug happy professor girl (in a bikini, I might add). I was reading, poolside, with iced tea and my sunblock, the new issue of my favorite magazine, *Glimmer Train*. I'd sent them six stories over the last years. I had six nice rejection notices. I needed tenure. I missed school. I missed teachers. I missed my friends. I read the magazine, looking for clues on how to be a better writer.

There was a story set in Australia. I turned to it, and the magazine showed a stunning photo of the author. The story was wonderful. It was painful and clear and the prose was beautiful—the writing just sailed into my heart.

Hmm, I thought. *Australia.*

Then, I looked back at the name of the author. Derek something … then I realized the buzzing in my brain wasn't from the chlorine, or the Texas sun, or the chemicals in the sun block, or the iced tea … Derek? Derek! DEREK?

I quickly flipped to the back of the magazine, and read the contributor note. It was our Derek. He'd been so bad. Now he was so, so good.

I couldn't believe it. How did he do it?

I read the rest of the issue. Hands down, his story was the finest, most original, most skillfully crafted in *Glimmer Train*.

Later that evening, I saw two more of his stories in two of my other magazines! Derek was everywhere. I felt a mix of envy and pleasure and delight. I'd known him when he was so bad!

Over the course of the next year, I saw Derek's work in a dozen magazines.

Derek had made it. He had stayed the course.

When I knew him, Derek didn't care about workshop politics. He wasn't easily distracted or thin-skinned or dissuaded.

He followed something inside of him, even when everyone around him was frowning, scrunching their noses, ignoring him, or looking away. He was taking it all in and spending his time working.

Recently I heard Derek received a two-book deal and a major advance and has a screenplay with serious interest behind it. He gets interviewed in major magazines, so we can all see how he works.

I feel humbled by Derek's story and ashamed of the way I acted toward him. But I also feel his story has made me a better teacher. It is my job to tell everyone that it doesn't matter where you start. If you stay with this writing thing, you will get better. If you stay with it and work hard and refuse to be daunted, you might get really, really good. If I can do it, you can do it. If Derek can do it, you can do it. People who are writers probably used to suck. It's hard to believe. But you get better by staying with it, by not letting your sucky work scare you too badly. Keep writing.

Derek has made me more patient with the very worst students in my classes. I give them the benefit of the doubt. You don't know where the next talent is going to come from.

Bad writing didn't scare Derek. He stuck with it. He's a great example of a common fact: Most successful writers don't start out as successful writers. Most people don't write beautiful interesting layered pieces until after they have been *sucking* for a few years, maybe a decade. Everyone starts out as a beginner. Derek did. I did. Successful writers know how to learn how to write. Successful writers develop a tolerance for sucking. They stay with it. They keep learning.

Bad writing doesn't scare great writers.

Here's another way to look at the same principle, the principle of practice.

Atul Gawande is a surgeon. He has a wonderful book, *Complications*, that explains how surgeons learn. Surgeons' learning is a bit tricky, because they are, of course, practicing on actual people. Learning implies mistakes will be made. Sometimes, surgeons make mistakes on us—especially beginning surgeons.

Writers. Surgeons. Why do we often think they should be perfect? It's pretty unrealistic. Kind of distressing (in the surgeon's case), but there it is. At first, we aren't going to be fabulous. We're going to do poorly, make mistakes.

For surgeons, it's life or death.

This is good to remember. Bad writing doesn't kill anyone.

About training new surgeons, Gawande writes, "To be sure, talent helps. Professors say that every two or three years they'll see someone truly gifted come through a program someone who picks up complex manual skills unusually quickly, sees tissue planes before others do, anticipates trouble before it happens. Nonetheless, attending surgeons say that what is most important to them is finding people who are conscientious, industrious, and boneheaded enough to keep at practicing this one difficult thing day and night for years on end."

Gawande the surgeon says that having a doctor trained as a sculptor would be great—he'd be really talented, no doubt. But, he'd probably be flaky. Those who are truly successful, long term, are those who are less talented.

"Skill, surgeons believe, can be taught," says Gawande. "Tenacity cannot. ... And it works. There have now been many studies of elite performers—concert violinists, chess grand masters, professional ice-skaters, mathematicians, and so forth—and the biggest difference researchers find between them and lesser performers is the amount of deliberate practice they've accumulated. *The most important talent might be the talent for practice itself.*"

I urge you to reread that paragraph again and again. Copy it out in your journal. Paste it on your dashboard.

It's those who stay with it, doggedly, like Derek, like me, who succeed. Not those who write a few fabulous pieces. Not those who stop doing it.

Psychologists call this the "willingness to engage in sustained training."

These same studies show that top performers—folks at the top of their field—hate practicing just as much as we do.

But, they do it anyway.

In the writing practice world, no one is going to have the wrong limb amputated. You aren't going to miss a flesh-eating virus or mistake the flu for typhus or a brain tumor for a migraine. How wrong can it really go, with you, your notebook, your pencil?

The hard question though, that stops so many beginning writers, is this: What's the point of doing something you aren't really that good at? What if you are one of those people who (a) doesn't get better, even with practice, or (b) can't will yourself to do it?

These fears stop so many writers.

And that makes me deeply sad.

What about the stories we're missing, those lives that are lost to oblivion? That is a kind of death, a kind of terrible loss.

I know it's hard to be mediocre, dogged, and to practice,

day after day. If surgeons can practice—with all the odds and ethics and high stakes—certainly we can show up in our writing rooms for fifteen minutes and humbly write down our words.

Isn't it funny that doctors have *practices*?

And so do we. Writers have to have an open *practice*.

No matter what.

Is it a matter of life or death?

ON YOUR PAGE: *Exercise 28*

Study the art of practice. This week, read a book about Beethoven, Shakespeare, or Georgia O'Keefe. Look at Chekov's letters or van Gogh's diaries. Read the surgeon's book mentioned in this chapter, *Complications*. Look in the appendix for a topic that appeals to you, and delve more deeply into your understanding of practice, genius, work, and play. Get more information on the nature of practice.

ON YOUR PAGE: *Exercise 29*

Okay, this one is fun (and perhaps frightfully easy). Set your timer for fifteen minutes. Get to your computer, or open a fresh page in your journal. Ready, set—go with your worst writing. Use hundreds of adjectives. Completely ignore your experience. Write about something far away that you know nothing about. Think hard. Have a ball, make a huge mess. What's your worst writing fear? That you are superficial? Go for it! Write that way! Scared you don't know enough? Write stupid!

This is a good warm up for a daily writing practice, too. Something you can do every day to clear the decks.

Dare to suck.

Chapter 15
Compost

COMPOST WAS SOMETHING I MENTIONED ON THE FIRST DAY of class one year, in passing.

Now, I talk about compost a lot.

On the first day of a class, I have all my students write three questions for me—anything they want to know—on index cards. Then, I draw the cards at random, a few at a time for a few weeks, and I answer. They ask me about my husband, children, my mother, my dogs. They ask me how much I write, and why, and if they should be writers. They ask me which books are my favorites. They have asked if the dress I was wearing on the first day is reversible, where I went to school, how many drafts I do, if I have done drugs, to reveal a dream.

Most often they ask: Where do you get your ideas?

Writers don't so much have ideas, I tell them. Some writers have ideas. Their books are important and good—Coetze has ideas, Gordimer has ideas, Sartre, and Murdoch, too.

But really, for most of us, the writing life is more like the sex life.

It's an urge, and it has a certain dampness to it. It's a desire, a thing you look at from the side, not directly staring. The writing is gentle and fragile—nothing like an idea which is sturdy and forceful and clear.

You don't want to just stare, gaping, at a beautiful, lovely person. You try to act cool. A little not-needy. This is how the writer relates to her material. She doesn't really get ideas for writing. Writing is more of a pulse, a throb, a thrum. It feels more like desire and less like thinking.

It's something you feed, this desire.

Here's how: Finding your material is just like maintaining a compost pile.

Slowly, over years, you take your best stuff out to a secret, hidden away place in the backyard, and you dump it there. You cover the pile. You can buy things to help digest it (therapy, self-help books, and art classes equal worms, enzymes, wood ash). But it will digest on its own, too. Without any intervention from you at all.

All my students come to me with a compost pile. If they are young, say eighteen, their compost pile might be fairly small and compact, though rich. What is vital to learn early in the writing class is this: Your best work is going to come from your compost pile. Not the neighbor's yard. Not television. Not your head, your thinking, your "idea" for a story. If you aren't working from compost, you are going to be spending a lot of time revising.

Anyone who survived childhood has a good, if small, potent compost pile. The compost pile, to be successful, as you may know, has to be kept covered—and most people have kept the lid on childhood. It has to be forgotten by the main brain, the idea-generating self. Most people have forgotten lots of childhood. Writers have to have a good "forgettery." That's part of making compost: Dump rich raw materials, build up a little heat, and neglect. Alchemy happens. Compost happens.

So many of my students want to write about *anything* but where they are from or who they are—*anything* but their own terrible, lovely, banal, fascinating lives. Say your day goes like this: It's Monday, and on Monday your neighbor leaves notes to everyone: *Please pick up after your animal!* You live in a small, ugly, boring town. You go to school or work. You obsess over your lover, and the annoying person at work. You play online chess, and eat turkey for lunch, and go to the mall, and then to a movie. You argue with your mother, and then you get ready for bed, and settle in with a good book, not doing your homework. This is your Monday. This is your life.

Instead of writing from underneath *that very life*, you turn in a story about a prostitute who likes businessmen. Or, a man in World War II who lives in Chicago and writes letters to the president. Why are you writing these stories, which draw as their source television and movies and ideas for stories?

Ideas kill art.

Compost feeds it.

Compost is dark, stinky, and messy.

It's not sex abuse, Mommie Dearest, the awful things that happened to you.

It's what happened to you, what *stuck* onto your soul. My main job as a teacher is to get students to write their compost; compost is where everything fascinating and good is. And it's under you. It's in the backyard of you. Stop going across town. Stop *importing* stories that aren't really yours. If you aren't dreaming down deep into your own history, your own passions, your actual true, real, daily concerns and obsessions and the shapes of your lived life, you aren't going to be able to improve as a writer. You have to start where you are.

If you are a housewife in Cuba, you write about that (*Cuba Diaries* by Isadora Tattlin). If you are stuck in a boring town of sniping, marriage-hungry matchmakers, you write about that. (All of Jane Austen.) If you are brilliant and grumpy in Minsk, if you are bored and slightly drunk in Dublin, if you are from the smallest town in the Midwest, you write about that.

You gotta know what your composted material is. Start with what you have lived through. Compost—both the backyard kind and the writer kind—takes about, what, a year, three years, some say seven, to happen. To ripen and mature. You might not be able to write about things that happened last week. Most new writers have the best, most rewarding early success writing from the layers of material they've walked around with for a few years. Years.

My compost takes *seven* years. It's seven years before I can remove my own need to present myself as the Beautiful Tormented Misunderstood Star of my own drama and get at something of the truth.

Compost is how many professional writers refer to their material. How many times have your friends, the ones who know you are a writer, told you, "That is a great story. You should write that!"

Or, more perversely they might say: "Well, that was horrible, that you were robbed/mugged/alone at your father's funeral, but, wow, you can write about it!"

My mother has said to me: "Do not write about us, please, I beg of you." Then, when I did, she said, "She writes about *us*." She says this very angrily. As though I am taking their photograph and stealing their soul. Which I hope I am. In some way, all writers write about their family. Writers are always writing about themselves. Sarah, the nineteen-year-old student of mine from a celery farm in Rockford, Michigan, who wrote the prostitute story, is trying to find her way to her compost. I wonder if she fears her life lacks adventure, if she fears people see her as a virginal Midwestern teen, sans experience, sans life. I think she's trying to write herself a better script. My job is to nudge her into the stinky pile she's been tending. She just doesn't notice what it is that obsesses her. She just doesn't believe her life, her actual life, can teach her what she wants to know about the world.

We are a tiny cluster of human beings. We write about that tiny cluster. The best writers are able to lumber down on a stepladder into this mucky, stinky, rich, fecund place—a place where the good stuff (eggshells, coffee grounds, onionskins, and paper) transforms into the stuff that feeds, that makes growth and heat and life. Have you ever read anything on composting? You are allowed to pee (but never shit) in your compost pile. You are supposed to water it, then keep it covered, so the requisite temperature can build, and the magic transformation can happen.

I can write about something, usually, well, seven years after it happens. Seven years is how long it takes for a board to become earth. If said board is in the right (dark, dank, quiet, moist) conditions.

Compost is your best stuff.

Compost is the stuff of writing.

If you are fourteen years old, your compost bandwidth is probably fairly narrow, and this is a great, great thing. You don't have to dig too deep to find great stuff. Focus softly— dreaming back, and down, and in—and feel your way gently into the darkest areas, the scariest, wormiest, messiest places in your life, and just start writing there.

When you notice yourself going back up into the thinking part of your mind, what do you hear?

> This isn't interesting.
> Who cares?
> What's the point of this?
> Joey will get mad if I write this about his tattoo and his
>   ex and the sugar cubes.
> I need to sound more like a Writer.

All those sentiments are your head talking.

Forget about ideas. The critic lives in your head. When she appears, go back to your pile. Say: *I'm messing around here. Leave me alone.* Don't listen to your head. Your material is down in, a vibration just below the level of thought.

If you are twenty-one, your compost pile has some pretty interesting stuff in it. At least three layers of rich, fecund material. And it's in your pile. Not in someone else's pile.

What I notice about the twenty-one year olds I teach is they really, really don't want to write about what they know, where they are from, how they see the world. They want to be anyone else but themselves. Because, I surmise, they fear that if they are themselves, then the chances are too good they will turn into their parents.

Compost!

What's your compost?

Well, to find it, you will probably want to practice; it's like panning for gold. You write (daily, I will keep saying daily).

Yesterday I started a new swimming routine because I want to do a triathlon. I hated the swimming. Then I did it again today. I was amazingly strong and swam for forty minutes without stopping. Delicious.

This is how the writing is. Rarely will you *want* to really sit down and do it. You'll want to want that.

To get at your compost, ignore the frenzy of fear and desire that surrounds the urge. *Call the person on the phone*, we say to wayward daters. Call the compost with your writing hand, your imagining mind. Just go do it. You won't want to. You'll hate it. It doesn't matter. Ignore all the thoughts that come up, urging you *don't go to the pile, don't get dirty, keep your clothes clean, stay inside, watch television*. Ignore all that.

Composting will not feel comfortable. Probably ever. Successful writers and successful athletes learn how to handily tolerate discomfort—there's a higher goal.

The sixtieth lap, the hundredth time you do it, you will say to yourself, *I'm from a small suburb in the northeast, with only white people, and my father is a bore, and my mother doesn't drink enough, and she says unkind things, and my bedroom looks like I really liked* The Simpsons *way too much as a child, and I have a collection of beer cans on my bookshelves, and this is my material!*

If you don't like your compost, live differently, so that in seven years you will have other material.

When you hit compost, you know. It doesn't feel like anything else. It doesn't feel like air, like an idea, or like soil, venting, or journaling. It doesn't feel like therapy or friendship. You will know. It's moist and meaty.

You'll know, and you will have the key to the rest of your writing life.

I have my students read each other's work, and one of the questions they have to answer, one of the very first, is this:

Did this story/poem/essay come from the compost pile this writer keeps?

If not, we know she has to bring in a new piece—a truer one—next week.

These are the questions I ask my students about their material. Can only you write this? Are you writing from your lower heart, your thorax, not your head? Are you layering your obsessions in your writing or avoiding anything dealing with what you know and fear? What are you afraid of? It's right to be afraid—anything that is going to feed honest art damn well better be intense enough to be scary. Are you trolling for the richest, funkiest stuff you have available to you? Or are you wondering around the glossy plastic mall of life, skimming off the top, writing fake, writing ideas?

I think on the first day of a class, my students are trying to ask me the same questions, in their own way. *Who are you, are you for real? What makes you tick? What are you about?* This is what we all want to know.

It's why we read.

Your job: Write what we want to read.

In trying to teach my students how to get juicy, hot, and layered, I stumbled on the phrase *compost pile*. They started using it, and now I do, too.

ON YOUR PAGE: *Exercise 30*

To access your compost pile, you need to enter a trance state. You need to float down, and feel your way to sensory images that have power for you. Feelings, dreams, urges, sensations, memories, hunches, discoveries—these open the path to the place art comes from. Ideas, directives, theories, intentions ("I want it to be like this," or "I want to write about ..."), these all come from your head—not the place art comes from—and all will delay you accessing the material that you are destined to write.

Ideas are good for sermons, formal essays, school, speeches, and planning a garden.

To grow stuff, you need black gold: compost. It's damp, it's rich, it's dark, it's complex, it's covered up.

If you are like most people (scared of new experiences, unsure of this whole approach), you will need a few tricks to get into the trance state. To enter a trance state, which will allow you to float down to your art-worthy material, you might:

* *Read poetry for thirty minutes.*

* *Pray or meditate in a quiet room.*

* *Turn off the lights, light a candle, open a journal, or click on your computer and open a new document (turn off your computer screen). Write what you hear in your mind for twenty minutes.*

* *Listen to baroque music or hindu ragas (see the appendix for a terrific book on a particular method using music, the proprioceptive process).*

* *Take a quiet walk and come back and write.*

* *Get in bed and lie there and stare at the ceiling for fifteen minutes.*

Every writer finds her own tricks for inducing trance. Usually, too much attention to the method, too much "structure," or too much talking about it will "kill" the magic. See why I say developing a relationship to writing is so like creating a relationship with your lover?

Once you are in the trance state, you are ready to write, to delve into your "composted materials." Don't think! Stay open.

Here are some prompts if you get stuck or dry:

Describe the last time you felt shame.

Write a time when you felt both completely right and terribly wrong.

Write from a time you had to take sides.

Write from the point of view of the most annoying person you have ever met.

Write from the point of view of yourself the last time you were in the wrong but still steadfastly refused to acknowledge it.

Make a list of paragraphs covering every single thing you could not put on the memoir of your life because they would be too embarrassing, too hurtful to other people, too illegal, too shameful, too bizarre, too unbelievable, too immoral, too idiotic, too boring, too small-town or small-time, or too upsetting.

Tips for Success
Practice getting a feel for what thrums and what comes from your head.

Let yourself write badly, poorly, sloppily, weirdly. Think compost, not fine flowers. This is your raw material. Let it be raw, rough around the edges.

Chapter 16

Dreaming Deep

There are so many books on dreaming, creativity, and the way artists work.

To people like my father, my boss, and my teenage sons, these books are filled with a bunch of made-up wack-job cracked platitudes. *Dream your way to brilliance! Sleep and grow rich! Feel it, man, don't worry about knowing!* My dad thinks only artists don't pay their bills on time. My boss thinks it's impossible to be creative and also orderly, happy, and productive. My kids think all art is abstract, and artists are pulling a kind of grand scam on the rest of us.

If we take the time to really look at productive, interesting artists and how they work, we can observe qualities that are common to all of us—dads, bosses, kids, artists:

1. There seems to be an intellectual and spiritual place *common to all of us* where the stuff of art and the interpretation of human experience is nourished and realized.

2. Getting to that place requires a kind of contradictory habit of mind: complete focus and total abandon. Both of those, at once!

Yeats writes about it. Keats writes about it. Einstein describes it. So do Nolan Ryan, Martha Graham, and Michael Jordan.

Athletes call it the Zone. Sales geniuses call it rapport or communication. We all know it: *Things are going well, everything's clicking, work is suddenly effortless!*

Writers often call the process getting into flow or dreaming deep. You are awake, but you are in a kind of artistic coma, a trancelike state. Understanding this psychological aspect of our work is vital—much more important than understanding prosody, versification, and the principles of Aristotelian drama. Those things are all important. But they are secondary.

Dreaming deep is such an important concept for writers to master that it deserves, I think, more time—more time in the classroom, more time at readings and talks, more time in the texts we ask our students to read and study.

Writing is basically climbing up a giant mountain—it's a ton of work, stuff falls on you, you have to go to the bathroom, you have to carry a lot of baggage, in addition to self-doubt, and you probably didn't prepare enough. You can write essays, books, articles, sermons—anything this way. It's thoughtful, and you push yourself.

But to make art—something that will speak to someone maybe always and forever, maybe in deep ways, maybe not, but something that has more than regular old hiking/huffing/puffing/essays-for-school writing.

You have to dream deep, and dreaming deep means:

* You hike up the mountain. But when you get to the top, you have to fall backward off that mountain.

* You have no net, no assurance that your fall won't kill you, that this work will be good/published/read/finished/successful in any way whatsoever.

* You might land on very painful shards of evil pointed
  things. Equally as scary: You fear you might never land.

Dreaming deep means you write from your composted
place, for as long as it takes, and you can never know if you
did it right or not!

You can see why a lot of people say, "I want to be a writer."
But they don't write very much.

Writing is very risky. Not for the timid.

But nothing in the world feels better than falling backward
off that mountain everyone else is laboring to climb and free-
falling out into nothing—trusting the secrets you do know will
mean something to someone else, making their climb richer
and easier, and their view more thrilling and spiritual. It
means that you are not a hiker. You aren't camping out at
Base Two.

You are more like a bird or a sky.

It's this kind of fear—driven manic aplomb that makes
some cultures (oppressive regimes) execute artists before
anyone else.

Art is dangerous.

And you can make art.

You have to tell the truth. You have to learn a new method.
You will not want to learn this method—there are sentries pro-
tecting your compost pile, your unconscious, and they are
determined to keep you sane and safe and employed and fed.

You have to sneak past the sentries.

You fall backwards into your material. You dream your way,
just like when you were a kid, and you drew, or played with toy
soldiers or Barbies. Learning to write is learning to concentrate in the same way you did when you were a kid playing.

In order to develop your writing muscle, you need to move out of your conscious brain ("I have an idea for a story!") and into your unconscious dreaming brain, where all the good stuff is waiting to come out.

To distract your thinking mind, you need to busy it. Driving a car, reading poetry, taking a shower, taking a walk, doing the dishes—all these help, as you have probably noticed, to clear your mind, and, when you are engaged in these activities, real juicy stuff sometimes pops up.

Today, simply notice your mind. Can you distinguish between your waking dream state and your thinking mind? It's hard, because now you are engaging a third part of your brain, the one that watches the other two!

As you go through your day, carry a notebook. Whenever you can, stop, and notice—what was I just thinking? Jot down what you were thinking. Try to notice how quickly you go back to the front of the mind, when you put pen to paper. How quickly you get writerly, start editing.

Practice knowing your own mind by simply watching it, as you would if you were doing a science experiment or painting a landscape.

Today, notice your mind at work and play. Your job is to capture it when it is free-floating, at play—not being driven by the sentries or trying to please your mother or your teacher.

Chapter 17
How to Be Unpopular and Why

I LOVE WHAT ISABEL ALLENDE SAYS ABOUT WRITING: NO complaining about how hard it is to write, we are all so, so lucky to write, to sit down, inside, and write words on paper—there is no greater freedom, no greater good, nothing that brings more joy. She is absolutely right, and I have tried to stop complaining about how hard writing is. It feels a little obnoxious. Writing is a luxury. You sit indoors, usually. You put words on paper. Pretty good deal. You are free. Writing is joyous.

But, everyone forgets this about writing: It's really tiring. You will be worn out, the same exhilarating exhaustion you have after running three miles or playing with kids for a few hours or cleaning your house. Writing is great work, and it's hard work.

You know how when you aren't engaged with something, it drains you? Working in a meeting with people you don't adore on a project you don't fully believe in leaves you feeling anxious, cranky, tired, and restless. But when you hang out at the coffee shop with your three best friends, you can talk for three hours and leave feeling filled up, energized, creative.

There are two kinds of tired, two kinds of work. There's the drain that comes from activity where you're not giving your full self. Then there's the exhilarated, "good" tired that results after intense, hard-but-wonderful work. To listen to three friends talking for three hours takes a lot of concentration and enthusiasm. But the whole time, the friends (and the coffee shop) are feeding you. Deeply.

Writing is this kind of hard work. You will need to be rested to do it well. I have a number of colleagues who think poets are self-indulgent. I even have friends who think poets and writers laze around, musing, penning their poems, indulging their emotions, having a great old time.

Well, no.

It's really hard to write—most people I know who do it well can only work with the complete creative focus that art-making requires for about two hours. Two hours at a stretch, maybe two hours all day. The rest of the day, they revise, read, do other kinds of work, but pure writing, the actual writing, two hours, max.

I can shovel my driveway for almost two hours before I'm exhausted. It's about the same for me and writing. Doing something that takes a lot of focus or brute strength is going to wear you out—and two hours is something to be proud of (if you are totally focused and working)!

You can also go through the motions of anything—relationships, ditch-digging, sewing skirts, making dinner, raising kids—and feel always a little tired. A little unfulfilled and vaguely unhappy.

When you run a 5K race, you don't stay up all night the night before. You eat right; you go to bed early. When you have a big presentation to make or an important trip to take, you prepare yourself. You rehearse in your mind how well it's going to go. You pack the stuff you are going to need the night before. You prepare yourself especially for the next day.

Writing asks the exact same kind of preparation of us. You can't expect it to go well if you haven't prepared your body and your mind. You have to rest before you write. You have to be fed (stomach with protein, head with books). You have to be really ready to write. It's not something we readily admit in our culture, that writing takes enormous focus and concentrated energy and true stamina on a number of levels. I mean, there you are, sitting at your desk, looking out the window. Doesn't look like hard work. Looks kind of lazy, in fact. Like a big, fat waste of time.

Don't be fooled by the careless assumptions of nonpractitioners.

You might not be writing as much as you want to because you have an unrealistic perception about how much energy it takes to produce good writing.

For me, doing good writing is as hard as preparing a presentation for work. Every day. I have to be that focused, that collected, that on top of a bunch of details, that nervous and that excited, that pumped, and working that hard. That's what my life is like. A full-blown PowerPoint presentation for the ten top people in my company, every morning, straight, for two hours. Truly. Day after day after day.

I get ready every night. I pack for the trip. I load my dream mind, hoping I will wake in the morning inspired, clear, and refreshed. I read good books. I have my journal by my bed. Every night, I'm getting ready for my writing morning. I point myself that way.

Writing is physically and psychologically the most demanding work I do. If I am sleepy, I can't write. If I am distracted, drained, worried, fearful, hungry, thirsty, exhausted, or ill, I find it extremely difficult to write. If I am not prepared, in a kind of sly, unconscious way, I don't write. If I am not strong and aware enough to battle the judges and demons and critics who want to derail me, I won't stay with the writing for more than five minutes. If I ache, I can't do it. If I am overwhelmed by my day job, I find it really, really, really challenging to clear my mind, and my desk at home, for my writing life. Very hard work. Very hard. Nothing in my life—raising kids, being in a marriage, having old and ill parents, wintering in a town with no sunlight—is as hard as writing.

So, what is the solution? How in the world do you rest enough and create enough time for preparation, so you can come to your writing time ready to work, hard?

You become unpopular.

In order to carve out the time you must have for writing (and recovery and preparation) you say no. To lots of people and lots of stuff you're told to do.

My friend Betsy is a great shining example of a person who understands what it means to train for something—that there's a lot of no-saying involved. Betsy ran the Boston Marathon (and did really, really well). Betsy is also a writer. When her writing is going well, she is using the same methods for preparation and recovery (aka saying no to a lot of people and yes to herself) she uses for her sport.

Some of my friends sleep with novels under their beds. Betsy is one of these people. She has written three. They aren't great; she'll be the first to tell you. They were her learning novels. The new one though, the young adult book she has just finished—it's good. Really, really good.

Betsy also has ideas. Lots of them. She's brimming over.

She writes every day, all the time, in her car, after her son's piano lessons, while he sits in the way-back drawing comics. During dinner, she will get up to write down a word or phrase. Her husband likes it. (He makes really good bread from scratch, and is generally happy and in a good mood.) He wants Betsy to be the writer she has always dreamed of being. (Training Rule #1: Surround self with people who want you to succeed.)

Betsy has ideas for children's books. She's writing them up. She has ideas for a biography of a North Country woman. She reads her essays on the radio. She maintains a writing practice by going to the library twice a week and staying there for four hours, writing her poems and stories by hand.

Betsy has a really great writing life. She's doing it, a little bit, every day, always writing, never not writing, and she takes care of herself. She gets to bed early. She eats good food (that husband of hers).

But guess what. In order to do this, Betsy has had to remove herself from the contest called Most Popular Girl in Town.

Betsy comes late to dinner parties if she is writing hot. She skips important school-related events if she changes her mind about going and decides instead to stay in the library to write. She doesn't go to all of her son's play performances. Because sometimes, opening night is enough.

Betsy says no a lot. She also says, "We might be there, we might not." She leaves room in her life for training—preparing and recovering. Those two hours of writing time a day take a lot of attention during the other twenty-two hours. Betsy's secret to writing success is this: She knows it's hard work. Like training for a marathon. Betsy wisely conserves her energy.

Like Betsy, I have learned to put my writing-training first, and I am so much happier (and better published). I say no to students who want to talk, at great length, about their work. "No text, no talk," my teacher Jerry used to say. Talking is much easier than working. You can talk when you are exhausted, when you are digging ditches, when you are drunk. You can only work when you are rested, focused, and ready. My children self-feed. My students self-write. My colleagues can happily live without my presence at many, many meetings. I'm a writer. Even when I'm not doing it, I'm getting ready to do it. In order to keep my focus, I can't run for Miss Popularity. I have to think like Betsy.

Betsy is preparing not just for one long-distance event (the next marathon), but two (her next novel), and so she has constructed a life that makes room for the real work of these endeavors.

Here are some of the things Betsy has found unnecessary:

1. Errands. Betsy doesn't do errands. It's a policy she has. She is in training, and errands don't fit into her training schedule or help her reach her goals—running marathons, writing novels. It's amazing what happens when errands don't get done: nothing. Many things simply don't need to be done. We create these whole lives in our minds, but they aren't really the lives we want to lead. Try it for one week. Run no errands. What happens?

2. Complaining about work. Betsy doesn't complain about her work. Complaining about work at work is half the fun of going to a workplace. Complaining bonds us to our peers. Betsy doesn't do it. It distracts her. Betsy stays

focused on writing or running. If you withdraw from the pleasurable, slightly addictive cycle of discussing other people and their problems, you will be less popular. This conversation is also an energy drain.

3. Arriving on time. Betsy comes over when she can and she leaves when she gets tired. This is very annoying to many people. It's also brilliant. Betsy is one of the few people I know who actually realizes it's she herself who will wake up tomorrow, and she wants to be fresh for her writing, her kids, her running. In this way, Betsy puts Betsy first. If you invite Betsy to dinner, she will show up when she gets there. (She has come to my house more than an hour late for a meal.) I wish I could do this. I can't. But, Betsy gets her novels and her marathons done. She's a great mom. She sings at church, acts in community plays, reads to the blind. She isn't at all selfish. She chooses.

Why be unpopular? Why say no so much? You need the time. Writing is a long-distance event. You do a little bit every day. You aren't suddenly going to get gobs of time, the huge grant, a different life. This is it. And you can do it. You need the habit of No.

Instead of dreaming of some nirvana writing life, why not start writing now? Start training today. Perhaps, if you allow yourself, as Betsy does, to admit how hard writing is, maybe it will be easier for you to justify getting to bed earlier, easier for you to say no.

You might not want to live like Betsy—refusing to do little errands, showing up late, not chit-chatting in the kid pick-up line, skipping boring stuff. But she is one of the best examples

I know of a working writer living a regular life. A writing life is a long-distance runner's life, and you have to take care of yourself just like high-level athletes do. You don't have to be a great, fast superstar in order to run the Boston Marathon. But you do have to train. You do have to rest. You do have to conquer your head. You do have to be a little selfish, enlist the support of your friends, and risk being unpopular and maybe even uninvited.

In running, the hardest step to take is the one over the doorstep. You can then run for hours.

In writing, the hardest step is getting to your chair. Then, once you do, you have to stay put. For hours. It's physical, and it's intellectual, and don't let anyone tell you otherwise.

You can't run a marathon if you are sick and whiney and mucousy. You can't train for a marathon if you are driving people all over town every forty-five minutes or addicted to RuneScape. To write a novel, you have to train. You can't miss training for weeks at a time and compete/complete.

Your training comes first.

I see the people in our community supporting and praising Betsy for her running. I don't hear the cheers for her writing. In church, everyone clapped for her the Sunday after the marathon. What an accomplishment! It was a really neat moment.

But when we finish a novel, do people clap publicly? I don't think so. I don't see it. (Except in a few glorious places, such as the National Novel Writing Month organization—check out their Web site at www.nanowrimo.org.) Instead of celebration for working writers, I hear a lot of sniping, "She wants to write. Thinks she's a writer." I hear people say things about new writers in the tones reserved for sentences like, "She wants to become a spoiled princess." Or, "He plans on making a trip to Venus soon."

It's hard to tell everyone, "No, no, I can't, sorry because … I'm writing." It might be easier, a little, to say you are running in the evenings, in training for a marathon. The seas parted for Betsy, marathon runner, as much as they ever will. Maybe you—at the start of this new life, your real writing life—should say you are in training, too? Because you are, aren't you?

I suggest telling bald-faced lies.

This is unpopular-making, I know.

Think about it, though. What if you carved out ten hours a week by saying you were in training for a marathon? Would the people around you support your activity, your goal? What would gain their support? Why not tell that as the truth? Isn't it close enough? You might want to look at your writing life as a kind of a sport. Something you do for yourself, for fun, for relaxation, for a challenge. Something that feeds you, and keeps you healthy and able to give more to the people you love. You don't even have to say what you are training for. Do you?

Once you start saying no, you'll get addicted. Once you start showing up for your daily writing, you'll hate missing it.

You might love saying no. It's like olives. It's an acquired taste. It's not easy to pop that round odd thing into (or in this case, out of) your mouth. But as you grow up, some things you didn't like, because they're strong, become absolutely delicious.

Practice using no as a complete sentence.

You need to protect your writing/training schedule. But first, you need to believe your sport helps keep you alive.

Write down everything you have to do today. Next, write down everything you have to do this week. Try to fill the whole sheet of paper
with big and small and necessary things. What's on your list? Order
the kids' school pictures? Pick up the dry cleaning, get to the grocery
store, get gas, send memos to Joe and Alada, turn in receipts, figure
out something to do with the taxes? Now, take that sheet of paper
and burn it. Truly. You can rewrite your list later—you aren't losing
anything. But the fire you make is a powerful invitation to your sub-
conscious. Your frightened writing self-in-hiding will feel lured by the
flames.

Next, make a list of topics and titles and subjects—everything
you've ever wanted to write down or write about. Name novels, a
dozen. You are a prolific writer; you are unstoppable. Story titles,
poem topics, journal entries you would write if you only had more
time. Baby's funny sayings, the trees in the park across the street, a
novel about your father, a memoir about your mother, the book about
your fantastic lesbian sister.

Write down everything. Don't think. Don't worry if you don't really
have a giant list of things you want to write—that's perfectly normal.
Simply write down words you like a lot—impenetrable, nuance,
plucky. Don't try to fill up the whole sheet of paper, but do keep your
hand moving. Trees, motherhood, being a guy, my first girlfriend,
boredom, money, Anna Maria Ball and her flute-playing, going to
church, couches, cars, love, secrets, a plate of perfectly cooked eggs.
Write down everything.

Frame this list. Or at least paste it on your fridge or the bathroom
mirror. (I know you didn't really burn your to-do list. Go do that now.
I dare you.)

Think of something you did that was hard. Having a baby, getting a job, helping your parents, making the varsity baseball team, learning how to ride a bike. Now, divide a piece paper into two columns. At the top of the first column, write that hard thing. Then below it, list all the steps it took to achieve that goal (taking Lamaze, practicing after school every day, listening to your mom cry). The order of the steps doesn't matter—just try to write all the tiny actions you performed in order to complete the hard thing.

At the top of your second column print the words: My Writing Life. Jot down corollaries for each of the steps from your first column. For example, if your hard thing was "made corporate softball team and won championship," some of your tiny steps might be: "learned to hit ball toward third base" and "saved money for cool uniform." Your second column might have corresponding phrases such as "learned to sit at my computer for ten minutes at a time," "bought three reams of white paper on sale," and "wrote five single-spaced pages in one day."

Note: The writing column items can be made up. They need not have happened yet. They can be dreams or goals. But write them as if they have already happened to you. Make them tiny steps, and ones you would like to have happen.

Chapter 18
Passionate Irritation

HAVE YOU NOTICED HOW THINGS WILL BE SAILING ALONG, you feel lucky and good, and then *pow*, you get socked with a run of bad luck, a cluster of little disasters?

Last week, I was having a great week. Then, on Thursday, in class, a crying student challenged me to stay true to my goals, to walk away from drama. I failed the challenge. I was extremely irritated at the sobbing student. I spent too much time carrying on to my friends about how hard my life was. I got sucked in, off track, busted.

Dramas are seductive. It's so easy to spend all this energy thinking about other people's lives and needs and complaining inside your head about how hard they are making your life. This dynamic is a large contributing factor to the reason so many words don't get written down.

We need your words. We need your story. We don't need to hear, so much, about the bad day you've just had. We do need you to sit quietly in a room for two hours. Save the drama for the page.

Right in the middle of class. We were working, and she started mucousing all over the place. We'll call her Gloria. Her story—the one we were working on—was about a woman who restores cathedrals in London while educating the reader on being humble in the face of British history. The class said they didn't really believe the story. They didn't believe "art restorer." They didn't like the tone, they said. It felt like a bad art history lecture.

Gloria got significantly, hugely huffy. Her two friends in the class huddled around her and said to various class members: "You don't know a thing about London. We *lived* there last semester. If you'd *been* there, you'd know."

The hovering friends also said, "Gloria is in a play. And very busy."

Gloria broke in. "I'm in the play. I live at the theatre!"

"Well, one thing we do in fiction is let the reader feel smart. Like she knows a lot. You have to set it up," I explained, "so the reader feels one step ahead. Like she has access to all the information. It's not about the author. It's about the reader."

Everyone just stared at me. Gloria flung herself down on the table and wept in her large awful quivery way.

I felt horrible. I couldn't stop thinking about how badly class had gone. I couldn't resist: I called friends. I told them. Three days later, I was still telling it.

"This is good," Natalia said, when I told her the story.

"It's not good," I said. "I'm making the students cry. It's bad!" (See how we do this? Exaggerating, taking blame, making a little drama in which we are the star?)

"We just said the other day, we weren't going to do this any more. You have this whole writing life going, we both have been doing such a good job of saying no, and making that little word be a complete sentence. But here's the thing, this is the world saying, 'Are ya sure?'" Natalia sounded very happy with her diagnosis.

I was very unhappy with it. Even though it sounded exactly like something I would say.

I noticed I thought her idea was *really wrong*. That would be resistance. The very definition. If you hate it, there's bound to be something there you need.

It's easy to write when everything is going great. The true way to improve as a writer is to go to your practice when you are in the midst of a terrible crisis. (If you are thinking the Gloria crisis doesn't really sound very bad, you are exactly right—it wasn't. Aren't most of our terrible dramas really not, at all, anything?)

I didn't really want to spend any more of my time analyzing Gloria. She was just a student being a student. I teach, she students, end of drama. I didn't need to "figure" this out.

And I need to conserve my drama for use on the page, not the stage that is my classroom.

I quit talking about work. I got back to my novel.

A couple of weeks after the giant cry-fest, Gloria came to my office. She said, "The class hates me."

I looked in her eyes. I could see she was angry and righteous.

"You know what?" I said. "You are right. Do you want me to tell you why?" I was nervous, but emboldened. I knew this was the truth, and she hadn't heard it, or listened, before.

"Yes," she said, and she burst into tears.

"Listen," I said, patting Kleenex into her shaky hand. I told her, making my voice soft and calm, to stop talking about the damn play all the time and how hard her life was, and start asking people questions about their lives. I told her never to mention London ever again.

She started to argue. "I feel like I'm getting the 'play nice with others' lecture," she sobbed.

"You are," I said. "That's a perfect name for it!" I smiled. When she got up to leave my office, I told her I wanted her to write down everything we had discussed. That I was going to ask her on Thursday what I had told her. And that she'd better know.

She surprised me by saying okay.

And she surprised me by knowing on Thursday.

And being *perfect* in class. For the rest of the semester. Her last story submitted to the workshop was honest, and polished, and good.

Change your focus. Talk about life less.

Write your stuff.

Keep the drama in your art.

Keep your mind calm for creating. Don't get sucked into other people's problems.

When you have a series of great writing weeks, don't get alarmed or shocked when you run into a difficult situation— that's going to happen. Keep your wits about you. Remember, you are in training. You have to take care of yourself first, so you can write.

Ultimately, it's in your writing that you are going to feed others.

You really are.

Value yourself and your writing life enough to protect it from assault by the rough edges out there in the world. Saving yourself for your writing is, I believe, a holy and ultimately selfless act. Absorbed into the little dramas of daily life, that's what's selfish.

It's easy to be calm and strong when things are going well. When you are resting and exercising, your writing life is easy. It's when things are hard that we forgot all our tools. I want you to rewrite a scene. Literally. I want you to take a conflict, one that you obsessed on, blew out of proportion, talked about a lot. Something at work, or in your family or friendships—not life or death—but an irritation you spent too much time on. (It should be easy to think of one because we all do this many times each week, giving minor irritations—at the grocery store, in traffic, waiting in line longer than we deemed appropriate—way too much power over our imaginations).

I want you to rewrite the scene, actually putting pen to paper. Write yourself, your character, with your head in the clouds, the art space, the spiritual center. In the writing, react as your best possible self. Write the scene. Take all the drama out.

A FAMOUS WRITER CAME TO MY CLASS AND "HELPED" MY students with their work. He told Andrea she hadn't suffered enough to be a writer. That she was too young to write a memoir. He told her to give it up.

The next class session, my students were out of their minds.

I stopped them. I said, "Listen. If he were a really great teacher and an evolved person, how would he put this exact same sentiment? Does it sound like anything else we have ever heard?"

The class stared at me. Andrea was red and flustered and staring at the ceiling.

I kept going. "Andrea can learn from this guy, even though he didn't mean to teach her," I said. "I think what he really meant was one of two things. Andrea, are you brave enough to write? If you are scared of this jerk from New York City, you aren't brave enough to really tell your story, you just aren't. He is testing you. Unintentionally. Or, he's saying something I have said, much more politely. Write further back into your experience. Don't write last year, and don't write age three. Work on age fourteen. Steer towards your layered material. Move where shame lurks."

I trailed off. I was through trying to salvage something from the visitor's swath of destruction. "Here's the bottom line," I said to my class, drawing myself up straight and earnest.

"Andrea, your piece isn't finished. No, he didn't tell you this in a helpful way. But, the point is, you must keep working on this piece. You already knew that. Let's not be shocked and nervous and wilting. We can always learn."

Do you have to suffer wildly and be sixty years old and wise in order to write? How much do you have to *suffer*?

First of all, you have suffered. And, you did have a bad and instructive childhood.

And, yours wasn't the worst.

It wasn't *that* bad, because you survived it, and you are reading books on how to write. We're going to call it, with some degree of accuracy, the childhood you survived.

Regardless of how bad your childhood was, you are probably able to form supportive relationships (good for anyone who wants writing time), make reasonable goals, feed and clothe yourself, and find compassion for others.

If you didn't have a bad childhood, you are much better poised than the wrecked youth to set up and maintain a functioning writing life. You are, in so many ways, ahead of the game.

You do not have to suffer in order to be a writer.

The quality, pattern, and relative ease of your childhood—how much you have suffered, how old you are, how world-weary, world-traveled, world-wise—matter very little. You don't have to suffer in some world-class fashion. You simply need to notice how suffering works.

The bad childhood person may have a more acute sense of how people interact, because to cope, she had to watch, very carefully, for subtle signs that showed when the next emotional hurricane was blowing in. That can be helpful to a writer, the ability to pay close attention to the unseen movements and emotions in the human drama.

But the bad childhood person can also be a frayed bundle of self-hatred, doubt, enormously messy mental hygiene skills. She can be hard on everyone else, hard on herself, and not very good at setting up an orderly life, the kind that can support the rather significant demands of the artist's life.

Suffering doesn't matter. Awareness and insight about people matters. It doesn't matter what path you take to get to the place of awareness.

If you still aren't convinced, let's make a list.

Who are the writers with good childhoods? Well, we don't know! We don't know about Andrea's childhood or the famous man's childhood. We just don't—they don't even know. Some sociologists believe that happiness and suffering run along the same lines of intensity, whether you are starving and imprisoned, or bored and angry in the suburbs.

Your awareness of your personal myths, the fantasies you present about your past, your awareness of your weak points—that's what is important.

One brilliant, capable student, Evan, said after the famous man's fairly disastrous visit, "He was really a good writer. I liked the reading. He just wasn't very well socialized."

Thinking about whether or not your childhood was bad enough is a false question. It's barking up the wrong tree.

You can stop asking if you had a bad enough childhood.

You can ask instead, "How can I create a productive writing life today?"

Pondering your relative degree of suffering is a dead-end. It's a way of letting yourself down, by comparing your worth to other people's history. None of that matters. What matters is the ability to create a writing practice you return to every day. If one asshole gets you off course, you haven't created a good enough present yet, and that's what you should be focusing on.

Read the lives of the writers. Learn what contributes to the shaping of the artist's life. Watch other writers, by reading interviews and biographies, to see how they develop obsession, awareness, and the talent of the room. Practice sticking with it for ten minutes at a time. Developing a writing practice will teach you everything you need to know about suffering! It's this familiarity with failure and inability to maintain focus, to get thrown off your track, which will keep you steadfast under fire.

The jerk who questions your right to even write is all too common. He's going to visit Andrea again. In all kinds of different guises. Why is he so potent? Because he is the embodiment of your own worst fear. That you don't deserve to do this. So prove the devil otherwise.

The present matters. Insight matters. Not your particular past, and the drama of you in that past.

Andrea has suffered—too much *and* not enough. It matters not one bit. What matters: Did she focus on trying to tell the truth today? Is she keeping her promises to herself and the page?

And if you are worried that the cruel words of a famous writer could wound, permanently, the writer within, then you must write a glorious fuck-you letter to that wounding person. Prove him wrong by writing every single day for the rest of your life.

Become more famous, not less.

Write your childhood two times in thirty-minute timed sessions. This exercise is best done on a computer, fast. First, in thirty minutes, write an account of your childhood emphasizing (way out of all proportion) only the fabulous parts. Leave out everything remotely sad or imperfect. Make a huge deal out of all the idyllic situations—that the beach was nearby, you were always tan, your mother made a beautiful cake when you thirteen, you were the best kickball player on Buckwood Drive.

In one fast, binge writing session, write all the blessed parts.

Take a break.

Then, write the evil version. The bizarro version of your life. You can pretend you are suing your parents, or you are venting to your best friend or a sibling—your life was ruined in a hundred small and huge ways. Dramatize the worst moments, list wildly, present your same past, wearing dark lenses. Exaggerate the despair when you didn't make the football team; when Betsey blew you off; when your father didn't take you to Morocco; that you were born youngest, oldest, or middle. Write about when your dog died because you didn't fill the water bowl, you chewed gum through your entire confirmation, you looked at your grandfather's vintage pornography collection and lied, you sold your sister to neighbors when you were six, you peed your pants when you were eleven. Everything, every tiny thing, things you've never written about or even thought about—they all go in your thirty-minute terrible childhood.

Print out each version. Which was easier to write? Which was more fun? Do you see how both are true?

If you want to, take an incident from either version, and write it in a way that is mixed—some good, some bad.

That's how the truth of suffering is arrived at.

ON YOUR PAGE: *Exercise 36*

Write your dream childhood. Does this affect how you (will) parent?

ON YOUR PAGE: *Exercise 37*

Write letters to each of your parents (living or dead) forgiving them for a small and a huge thing. This can be a very potent exercise—be careful. If you feel you want to, answer the letter, using your non-dominant hand to write yourself, in the voice of that parent, after imagining he or she has read your letter.

Chapter 20
Three Years

WHEN I WAS A YOUNG WRITER, A FAMOUS WRITER TOLD ME that becoming a writer requires a ten-year apprenticeship. That I shouldn't expect too much to happen before three years—it takes that long to establish a meaningful writing habit. Another three to learn the techniques, get the benefits from the practice. And a final three-year chunk, he intimated, to put the habit and technique together, and learn the world of writing.

He was not very popular.

But here is what I have noticed. It takes three years to get your mind and your body working in concert. I think it's helpful for beginning writers to know that it is going to take a really long time to feel comfortable and be productive as a writer. It's not going to happen in fifteen weeks.

Some of my friends think this is depressing advice, and too discouraging. "You can do it!" they chant constantly. "You can do it."

But be realistic, too—you not only can do it, you have to do it. One day at a time, for three years.

Hard fabulous things take awhile to get good at. Piano lessons. Toilet training. House painting. Hair styling. Anything. You get better as you practice.

I have noticed there are three phases, that go in roughly three-year chunks, to taking on a new skill or habit of mind.

When I started running, I could never see past the end of the run I was on. I kept thinking the entire time that I would need to stop, very soon, or risk permanent damage to my hamstrings, ankles, and feet. I ached and hated it, every inch of the way. I "started" running for a couple of years, stopping before I got confident or could run for more than two miles. Starting and quitting, starting and quitting. Buying new shoes, then not running because it was rainy. A thousand and one excuses—you know them all. I had too much to do. Running is too hard on the body. It's a hassle to get all sweaty, then get showered and back at my desk, too much effort.

All the running timetables and programs and schedules and charts use fifteen weeks or twelve or maybe even eight. They get you running, like a pro, one workout at a time ... and voilà! Off you go.

These charts have never, ever worked for me.

It took me three years to seriously incorporate running into my life. To get to the point where I feel good about running, where I place in local races (never better than third so far), to where I would rather run than not run.

This is where I want you to get with your writing.

To the place where you would rather do it than not do it, because skipping a writing session is like skipping a workout. It's *harder* to start back up. If you are off for a week, that next Monday back on the StairMaster is living hell. If you are off for two weeks, you might even be back to walking first! Yikes! Three weeks off, you're toast.

Sometimes, it's too hard to start back up. It's easier to keep not doing it. Here's the truth: It took me a year of that kind of quitting and wallowing and not-sure-ness with running.

Same with writing.

I've been running for three years now. I call myself a runner now. But it took a long time for me to incorporate the sport into my life. The first year was all about resistance and fear and quitting and hating it because it hurt. Perfectly normal, but the running magazines and women's magazines don't tell you that. I think we're often set up for failure. I wish someone had said, "At first you are just playing with it. It's not going to be serious, it's not even really going to take. Keep going, though, the rewards are down the line."

I wish someone had told me to have very low, very realistic, and very easy to reach goals for my running. And for my writing.

This advice runs counter to every single writing book I have ever read.

It runs counter to everything I hear about changing your life.

But it's true.

It's going to take three years.

I see this as great news, not depressing.

I don't understand why more people don't want slow results. Fast results aren't results. They're just fast.

It's not popular to see gross, unabated failure as a crucial part of learning anything important. I think the ancients understood this. I don't think we let ourselves have enough time on our hands to learn. And I see a lot of very frustrated nonwriting beginners, feeling like they alone are the only ones who can't "get" it.

Give yourself three years! Please?

Year three is when the magic happens. And I wish I could

say all this will happen in "instatime," that you can have a fulfilling glorious writing career today if you really want it.

I believe it takes a couple of years to make something part of the fabric of your soul. For our bodies to take on the chemistry of another person, an activity. For dance or music or math or language to be in us, part of us, streaked all through our nature.

Year three is the first time—as a mom, as a runner, as a writer—I don't question my every move. It's totally a habit now, on all three counts, like breakfast. I do it every day—holler at the kids, jog two or seven or four miles, write my pages. I don't decide to do it, it's just something that is happening.

But it took me three years to get to this point. Not weeks. It took thirty-six months of not knowing what the heck I was doing or why, and many, many days of seeing myself as utterly and completely Not a Mom, Not a Runner, Not a Writer. Something else. But not that.

Give yourself more time.

Give yourself ten years to play with this endeavor called writing. Give yourself a much larger canvas on which to work. There's no deadline. It's too early to say. You won't know at the end of this year, or after doing fifty of these exercises. You can't know yet. You have to put in, I truly do believe, your *years* of falling off the horse. You have to get to that point in your practice where being miserable and quitting is less fun than doing it. That takes a lot of time!

Think in terms of years. You are going to be doing this your whole life. You have time.

Let your mistake-making period last longer, really long. Stretch out the whole process.

Make two writing programs. If you like, base them on those running or workout schedules, where you have to run *X* laps on Tuesday and lift *Y* weights on Wednesday. If you like spreadsheets, go for it. If you want to scratch these on the back of a cocktail napkin, more power to you.

In the first writing program, be rigid. You must write poems on odd-numbered days. You need a story a month. And, if you write one page a day, you will have a novel by the end of the year. Journaling is your warm-up, you need two pages, and then do fast writes as your wind-sprints (you will need that twice a week). Time off for recovery? Not needed. Diet? Books. Books, books, books—put all that in. How many pages you need to read? Program the heck out of it!

In the second writing program, do the opposite. It's a ten-year plan. What do you need to write this year? Be very gentle. No matter what your age, work on a ten-year scheme. Think in three-year chunks. You might put down something like, "Year one: get feet wet." In year two, maybe you will go to a writing conference, yes, that's it. That's what you will do year two. Journal, if you feel like it. Try writing every day over Christmas break—no, five days in a row. Sometime during year two, when you feel like it, you will write five days in a row. It's okay if you skip. It's year two. Very low expectations. Year three, you see yourself liking writing a bit. You think maybe in year three a short story will be completed. Yes. You can see that. Notice your body. Notice how relaxed you are?

Give yourself time.

Enormous gobs.

You have that.

Chapter 21
Little Loops

I KNOW LITERALLY HUNDREDS OF PEOPLE WHO WANT TO write. And they don't.

It's a cliché, and you hear football coaches and tennis players saying it all the time, but writing is a head game.

The first thing you might look at when you think about writing more—more pages, more seriously, more deeply—is your resistance. Most of us get caught in a little loop. We say we want to write. We think about what we want to write. We sit down, for a moment. We don't write so much.

What are the thoughts you have when you think about writing? Can you increase your level of awareness about the messages you send yourself? Can you stay with one thought long enough to capture it, pin it down with words?

Some of us think something like this:

I am going to write today/tomorrow.
I am going to start my novel.
It's going to be about _____.
I'm going to start by really writing, sticking to a schedule—
    writing a lot.
I'm deathly afraid my novel will suck.
I wish I were a better writer.
I don't want to completely wreck my novel idea by writing
    it just yet.

We begin what I call little loops.

Little loops are terrible. A little loop is like having popcorn stuck in your teeth.

On the first day in my classes at college, I always have my students fill out cards. I ask them things that I think up on my way to the classroom. I ask them what their dream writing project is. I say, "If you had unlimited talent, a five-hundred thousand dollar grant, and a cabin in Vermont, what would you write?" I ask them what they are working on, in their fiction, their poetry, their personal lives, as learning writers.

See if you can catch yourself going right into a little loop. It might take some practice. Getting to know how your writing mind works is absolutely essential if you want to write regularly, regularly enough to publish books or articles or finish a story.

Write down on an index card six to twelve words or so that anchor one of your writing ideas.

I wrote on my cards: *COMING OF AGE NOVEL, BLOSSOM, GRAVE, SET IN FLORIDA, GIRLS, COLLECTION OF ESSAYS ABOUT THE 80s.*

Whatever comes to mind. Just write.

Now read your card, and be ready to really think and feel. When you read your card (and you have to be quick, observing a little loop in action is exactly like catching a mosquito) pay attention: Do you seize up? Does your mind go a blank? After the rush of the first idea what do you *think* and *feel*?

The idea is to practice. It might take a bunch of cards. Keep writing down ideas, and then, swat around, flail wildly, move quickly, but stealthily.

Are you telling yourself:

Great card but it repeats what you've already written.
Great, but it's already been done.
Fine, but it's never been done, probably means it couldn't be.
I don't have time for that big of a project.
I don't have time for that insignificant of a project.
I'm not smart enough to write essays.
It's stupid, though.
Way beyond your reach. You haven't even written one essay!

I don't know what gets played over and over on your little loop. I do know that most people—writers and nonactive wanna-be writers—have ideas. Then they stop. They stop really early. They may let themselves continue by buying a book on writing, taking a class, daily journaling, making notes, starting, maybe, the project. But they don't finish.

And they don't know why.

Part of being a writer is paying extraordinarily close attention to what is on your mind.

Can you sneak up on your mind?

Mosquitoes are *attracted* to movement. It's how they know you are alive—fresh blood *moves*.

Can you quiet down, still yourself, and then, stealthy, steady—pop?

It seems so simple. It's not. Being aware of what you tell yourself to not write is a daily maintenance habit. It's like making your bed. You have to do it—be aware of the wrinkles— over and over and over.

I have listed a number of books in the appendix that I believe you will find helpful. But there are two books that are so insightful on this process—learning how to find the loops that keep you from fully starting and joyously finishing your work—that I have to tell you about them here.

Michele Cassou's *Point Zero: Creativity Without Limits* is written for visual artists. This is the best book for raising your ability and awareness to know the creating state of mind, when you are in it, how to get in it, what keeps you from being in it.

David Bayles' and Ted Orland's *Art & Fear: Observations on the Perils (and Rewards) of Artmaking* looks at why art gets made and doesn't get made, and the nature of the difficulties that cause artists to give up along the way.

I highly recommend you go to your library and check out these books, and others on the shelf near them. It's gratifying to know a lot of interesting people have been working on these problems—the ones *all* writers and artists deal with on a daily basis.

ON YOUR PAGE: *Exercise 39*

You need a deck of one hundred index cards. Buy them in a color that pleases you. Unlined is perfect for this.

And you already know what to do.

Grab a card. It's small. You are going to write in big capital letters. One writing "idea." Dream big—this isn't actually about the work you are going to do, it's about practicing your little loop management style. So, it doesn't really matter what you put on the card—pretend you are Stephen King or Flannery O'Connor or that your life is exactly how you want it to be—work from that imaginary place. (If you are working from your "poor little bad writing me" place, that's just as imaginary, you know.)

Put down a dream project. You have all the time in the world to write the project, but only a few seconds to write on your card—GO!

The flash I saw when I wrote a "mother" card was that there are all these bad books of mother poetry where the daughter complains about how hard she had it. I don't want to write that book. The flash had in it failure and why-start. On the back of the card, I write down those words, the cockroaches that came with the idea. This is not comfortable.

Keep repeating this exercise: *Lather, rinse, repeat.*

When you write something down and you can see the book whole in your hands, it's a mosquito-free feeling—there is nothing you can put on the back of the card but Ah. It's like conception. The whole world moves a teeny bit to the left. That card, you keep.

You can keep writing your same ideas over and over. This is a clearing process. Break the little loop by simply shining light on your thinking. Clear away the demons, and you will write that project. You have to see it, clear, first.

Chapter 22
Blocked

WRITER'S BLOCK IS A MYTH, AN EXCUSE, I USED TO TELL MY students. "Get over it!" I'd holler, when I was first teaching, waving my arms like a televangelist. "The writing will save you! The writing is the thing! Just put words down, anyone can do it. Just write. Write out of the block. Write under the block. Write around the block."

Got block? Lower your standards, I declaimed, quoting William Stafford.

I quoted all my favorite writers.

I had never been blocked.

I thought blocks were fake. Lazy.

Then I got blocked.

I was hired as a professor of creative writing, my dream job. All my writer friends and all my teachers had told me no one gets a job teaching creative writing, no one does any more. They all said I should find something else to do, something to fall back on.

Teaching writing *was* my Fall Back On thing.

I got, against great odds, the job, a great job, at a university. And I didn't write for three years.

I was miserable.

I was blocked.

I worked so hard to get the dream job and when I got there my new colleagues said exactly this, and I am quoting:

"Heather, you need a story in *The New Yorker*, a book of criticism on Zora Neale Hurston, and also the short story collection needs to come out from a press we have heard of. Not a podunk press."

I smiled whenever they said this, which they did in the halls of our building and also at most social occasions. For example, I was at a party at a colleague's house—my welcome party. She looked like a pussy willow—gray soft tufts on a hard reed. The poet said, "Heather, to keep this job you need a story in *The New Yorker* and a book of criticism. And you need the collection to come out, how is that all going?"

I smiled and nodded. I also felt myself dropping through a fissure in the poet's trendy cement floor, and into an oblivion I hadn't known existed. And though I knew it was irrational, I wondered, *Why do these people hate me?*

At the initial job interview, I'd said I loved writing about Zora. Which was true, I did. But not in a scholarly way—more in a way like how you talk about your neighbors, you know, that woman on the corner who has the coolest stuff and you want to know all about her life and how it got that way. Because in a way, Zora was that woman on the corner for me; my mother's house was a few miles from her original house in Eatonville, Florida.

That night after the poet's scary party, I went home to my small expensive apartment near the university, and I wept.

In the following weeks, I couldn't stop crying.

I tried to please the poet by doing dances at work—Teacher dance, Committee Girl dance, Helpful to the Secretaries dance.

I tried to write.

But I couldn't do anything in my apartment but cry. I tried writing in cafes. I couldn't do anything in cafes but weep—it was getting a little weird.

I started drinking white wine.

I started watching hours and hours of *The Mary Tyler Moore Show* reruns. Perky, splendid Mary became, through my wine haze, a kind of totemic figure.

Mary, Mary, Mary.

I got through each day with my students simply in order to get in bed and watch Lou and Ted and Mary and the newsroom. The show seemed, somehow, to explain everything.

I drank a lot of white wine. Way, way too much.

The poet said, whenever she saw me in my office, "Are you doing research? That is important. Don't spend too much time with those students. They can suck you dry."

I said my research was going fabulously well.

I wondered: *Could I write something on Mary Tyler Moore?*

Stories of mine appeared in print, and a book of poetry. Here's the thing: There is, as you may know, a long delay in the publishing world. Things I'd written in grad school won prizes and appeared in print, one and two years after the fact. (Oh, grad school! I missed it so much! My teachers who adored me! My friends who were allies and interesting and in it together! My little mobile home! My tiny car! My late nights writing papers—all of it seemed so far away and wonderful—why had I wanted to graduate a year early? I couldn't think why.)

Meanwhile, in Texas, I burst into tears at red lights for no reason. I yelled at a cashier at the grocery store because she rang up my broccoli as endive. I cried at an Italian restaurant because I was so hungry and the food never came.

At my annual review, I was praised for publishing so much, and cautioned—by the pussy willow poet and the scary department chairman in her bright Texas yellow suit, black blouse, nylons and yellow pumps—not to spend so much time in the office with students; I should be home *writing*. We want to see your research, they said. They nodded, like discerning, rigid mothers.

I am afraid I nodded back.

Shortly thereafter, in the afternoon, before my fiction workshop, I accidentally drove my car into a car while going forty-five miles an hour. I turned left on a green light on the perimeter road that curved around the beautiful campus. I was listening to Led Zeppelin and thinking about my student Ryan's short story, how the sister needed to come into the bar scene earlier, and that we needed to have the camera on her longer, slow all that down. I was seeing that scene-to-be-born in my mind, and I wasn't wearing my seatbelt. I don't know why I wasn't wearing my seatbelt.

I lay in the hospital. No one, not one person in the world, knew where I was.

No one visited me.

My face was changed, a lot. The smile—that fake caramelized smile—was gone. Scars ran from my ear to my lip, my lip was sewn on irregularly. My sense of smell was nearly gone, my nose had been severed much from my face. For a long time, it hurt to even open my mouth. Like all brain injured people, I had trouble reading, concentrating, remembering.

I was blocked.

And I couldn't write.

Big time.

In order to unblock, this is what I did.

I had affairs with inappropriate, wild, sweet men; smoked cigarettes; drank beer; and polka-danced. My three-year engagement to a professor in another state ended. I spoke more and more Spanish, drank more, drank less, and I moved four times. Moving to new apartments is a great way to try to get unblocked, it feels so productive, and you get to set up all those writing studios.

In order to unblock, I also interviewed for jobs, flying all over the country every week all spring, every spring.

And I wept. I was rigid, shut down, and suffering episodes of blindness, literal actual blindness. I couldn't read books.

It's important to make a distinction between a writing block, a nervous breakdown, fear of writing, and the lack of knowing *how* to write. They are each different states.

When you are truly a blocked writer, you have dedicated your life, your time, your space, your heart and mind to writing. You have studied writing, and you read constantly. You go to live readings, you live the writing life. And you can't write—physically, you are never able to get to the computer, the studio, the paper. That's a block. The energy that you would be putting into writing is there—you have that energy—but you can't direct it to the page. There's a block.

When your life is very upside down, you probably can't write—writing takes more focus and concentration than despair allows.

When you are *afraid* of writing, it's quite different than being blocked. When you are afraid, you really want to write, but you won't let yourself write. You don't have the energy for it. You are afraid of opening a vein, you are afraid of hurting someone or yourself, you are afraid you will suck and you are afraid you won't really suck, and that you will have to change your life in order accommodate this new thing, the writing life. You are afraid of the changes you will have to make in your life. You don't write.

Beginners who don't write but want to write aren't blocked—they're scared. Learning more about writing, and about what a writing life looks like, is the best cure for fear.

A block, I argue, happens to people who have been writing and then can't. After the first book is published, just before the novel is completed, during a summer of wonderful writing days, fall comes—the words dry up. A block happens to writers who are on a writing path. Fear can keep you from starting (and that's easier to fix—knowledge destroys fear). A block keeps you from going on. A block is a snarl of complex fears and anxieties. You have to go through the motions of your writing life, feeling dead. You have to keep reading, keep going to live readings; you have to pretend you are a writer. You can manage your block, you really can:

1. Don't cling to what you have written. Stay light. Start new books and write through to the end. Look forward by staying right where you are today. Don't look back.

2. If you are blocked, you might make terrible choices. Don't sign up for things that will cause you to be too far from the (great) person you are.

3. Construct your life so that you stay unblocked. Don't wait for a block (I almost died, literally) to learn how to remain unblocked.

4. Surround yourself with people who are already like how you want to be.

5. Write the books you want to write, not the ones you think you should write (see: Russian Lady).

6. Square your commitment to writing with your goals—is it realistic to want to write a novel if you can't figure out how to sit alone in a room writing (bad stuff) for one year, not missing many days?

7. Do not write alone. Writing is an activity that should be deeply fed by kind, loving allies. Find ways to make friends who are writers.

People who are blocked make terrible, terrible choices. When it comes to writing and to life, blocked folks unconsciously make choices that allow them to live out their fears. They take jobs where they will *never* get to be writers and then complain bitterly that their job doesn't let them be a real writer. They fear they aren't writers, that their words aren't important. They close their eyes and hope for the best.

I haven't worked on my novel for two weeks. Which in a novel's life is pretty much No Pulse Discernible. Tonight, I will start again. And this time, write through to the end.

I'm not blocked. I'm not afraid. I'm just busy.

It's important to know the difference. And, it's important not to let busy or fearful get too far along. They are infections that can get out of control quickly, and lead to a disaster. Beginner fear is normal, and it's not a block. Keep learning. If a block happens to you after you have got your healthy writing life up and running, you aren't alone.

ON YOUR PAGE: *Exercise 40*

What unfinished business do you need to take care of in order to
clear the decks of your life for your best work? Do you have marital
work to do? Work on your body? Do you need to quit your job, really?
Do you want to embark on a year of psychotherapy or take a dance
class? What do you need to do to get out of your own way? If there's
something big in your life that isn't being addressed, it's likely your
writing life will reflect that. The writing life really is like a kid.
Everything the parents say and do comes out in that kid. The
writing life is a like a mirror of your real life.

ON YOUR PAGE: *Exercise 41*

Have you ever been blocked? Can you see a time in your life where
you could be blocked? Write a story or a poem about a blocked
writer. Show how he creates his own block, builds it higher, and can't
see this very fact. A block isn't a bad mood. A block is laziness, or
procrastination—that's usually fear. A block is huge, and lasts a
long time, and is caused by something not related to your writing.

ON YOUR PAGE: *Exercise 42*

Read a book on blocks. See the appendix for some suggestions.
Spend a few days reading, and then write at least three days in a row.
That's a great way to cure, or at least massage, a block. If this is too
hard, enlist support! Therapists, friends, sports partners, spouses,
and children are all good for writing dates. You don't have to do it
alone.

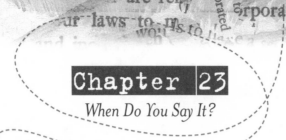

Chapter 23
When Do You Say It?

WHEN I WAS TWENTY-SIX YEARS OLD, I ATE WITH WRITERS, lived with a writer, read my work aloud at bars and coffee shops, read writers, went to writing conferences, traveled hours by car to hear poets, listened to tapes of writers, took writing classes, majored in writing, was working mightily toward a Ph.D. in writing, and I never, ever said, "I am a writer."

To say it or not to say it was much discussed among my group of writing friends. Mary Jane thought we should say it. "I'm saying it," she claimed. "We write," she said. "Writers are people who write. I write!" We thought Mary Jane was bold and wild. We worried she was wrong. She went around saying, "I'm a writer," when people asked her what she did.

We all wonder when to say it, who gets to say it.

To say "I am a writer" implies you have made a crucial move from the land of the knuckleheaded to the land of the brilliant, the famous. To say you are a writer was to say something akin to "I am a professional pitcher for the Atlanta Braves." You'd better really be on the team, or you sound pretty dumb.

But for writers, there aren't teams, T-shirts, draft picks, or playoffs. It's a little hard to tell.

When are you a writer? When do you get to say it?

Saying you are a writer—whether you write or simply desire to write—is seen in my family, my church, and even at my job

(where I am employed as professor-fiction writer) as preten-
tious, inferior, sad, selfish, and as unrealistic bragging. One
of Eudora Welty's oft-quoted characters says, "If you're so
smart why ain't you rich?" This is the same thing my uncles,
father, siblings, and students say to me, in all kinds of ways.

So I decided early on I would stay in the closet and let other
people call me a writer. On passports and customs forms, doctor questionnaires and legal paperwork, I list, always, my profession as professor, or, more likely, teacher.

That's what I'm paid regularly to do. (Margaret Atwood
wrote a terrific essay on money and art where she tells about
being asked, "Do you write the bestsellers?" "Not on pur-
pose," she says.)

So, are you are a writer? How do you know? When do you
say it?

Is it like losing your virginity? One day you are, then you
aren't? Can you be a little pregnant, a little bit of a writer?

How often do you have to *do* writing in order to keep
your claim to the title "Writer"? How many pages do you
have to write?

Once you are "out" as a writer, then if you stop writing, what are you? A former writer? A recovering writer?
A bad writer?

Another famous example comes from the kindergarten art
teacher. When she asks her students, "How many of you know
how to draw?" Every hand in the classroom goes up. When
twenty adults are asked the same question, one, maybe two
people will raise their hands, hesitantly.

I have been in rooms where no adults raised their hands.

My mom is a writer who doesn't write. My father is, too.

My father is at work on a multivolume novel-autobiography, a kind of Lawrence Stern meets Mark Twain. He has written a few chapters, here and there, over the years. I treasure each word.

My mother majored in journalism and went to work for the local paper, where, like women all over in the 1950s, she was given the option of obits or society page.

Both in their mid-seventies, my parents say to this day, "I don't have time to write. I wish I had time to write."

You can say you are a writer any old time. You can declare it so. You can declare it today. You don't even have to write. It is a thousand times better to say "I am a writer" and not write than to say "When I have time, I want to write." The first one is a potentially helpful lie, maybe a goal. The latter is a little loop that can lead you to much unhappiness.

Try this. Say it aloud (really, do).

"I AM A WRITER."

Really, say it out loud.

"I AM A WRITER."

Is it weird?

Now, say it this way: "I'm practicing writing."

Is that more accurate?

If you started saying "I write," what would change in your life?

When I was twenty-six, I said, for the first time, "I'm a writer." I said it aloud. I said it to a man on an airplane. I was feeling brave, as I typically do in airplanes, and I wanted to practice on someone I would never see again.

The man, in a firm suit, smirked at me, and said, "What have you written?"

This was the one response I dreaded most of all! I couldn't believe I had said this obnoxious thing. I felt withered. I was completely unprepared for his question.

"I write stories?" I said softly.

"Stories. About what," he said. The plane shuddered a little bit. I felt sick to my stomach. What was I doing? I was in way over my head. I could feel myself turning red.

"I don't know," I said after a while.

I was coming out. I couldn't answer his perfectly reasonable (I guess) question. But, I knew, suddenly and profoundly, something I hadn't really known before. I felt like shit, ashamed, and incredibly stupid. How was it possible I didn't know what I wrote about? I'd written hundreds of stories! None of that mattered. I sat there, a quivering mass of stupid red girl, and I knew: I wanted, very much, to be asked again. What do you do? I wanted to be asked again and again. I knew my answers, like my writing, would get better.

I knew I was a writer. At some point, it becomes impossible to deny it any longer. I imagine coming out is like this. It's a process. You get a little braver. Slowly. You test the water on strangers and in safe places. You can't deny it—your essential self comes out.

Becoming more conscious of the kind of writing self you're carrying around inside of you is a key step in creating a happy, delicious writing life. These exercises—try at least one—help you become more aware of the ways in which you have been a writer your whole life. Like kids who draw, naturally, you wrote, at one time, very freely.

Writing is in large part picking up where you left off. You'll be tempted to do the exercises in your head—and that kind of secret-keeping will probably delay your growth. You can't imagine love, you have to be in it.

You can't imagine your way through writing practice, you have to be in it.

ON YOUR PAGE: *Exercise 43*

Get your pen and some paper, and write—fast—for ten minutes on each of the following:

Write your art history—the story of your relationship to art and art making. What other activities—Building a house? Making the football team and playing well all season? Raising a child? Making cakes? Drawing floor plans?—prepare you for the loneliness and discipline of a writing life?

ON YOUR PAGE: *Exercise 44*

Write your autobiography in a list of the activities that absorbed you completely. The times when the clock stopped, and you lost all track of everything, except the activity at hand. Start from your earliest memory.

ON YOUR PAGE: *Exercise 45*

What do you need to have happen before you tell people you are a writer? Do you need to complete a novel manuscript, no matter how awful it is? Do you need to write every day for one month? Do you need to purchase a journal and a cool pen, but not rush to use it? What is "write" for you? Who is the most safe person you will tell? Who are the dangerous people to tell, the ones who might say they want you to write, but really, they will be afraid of what you could say? Make lists.

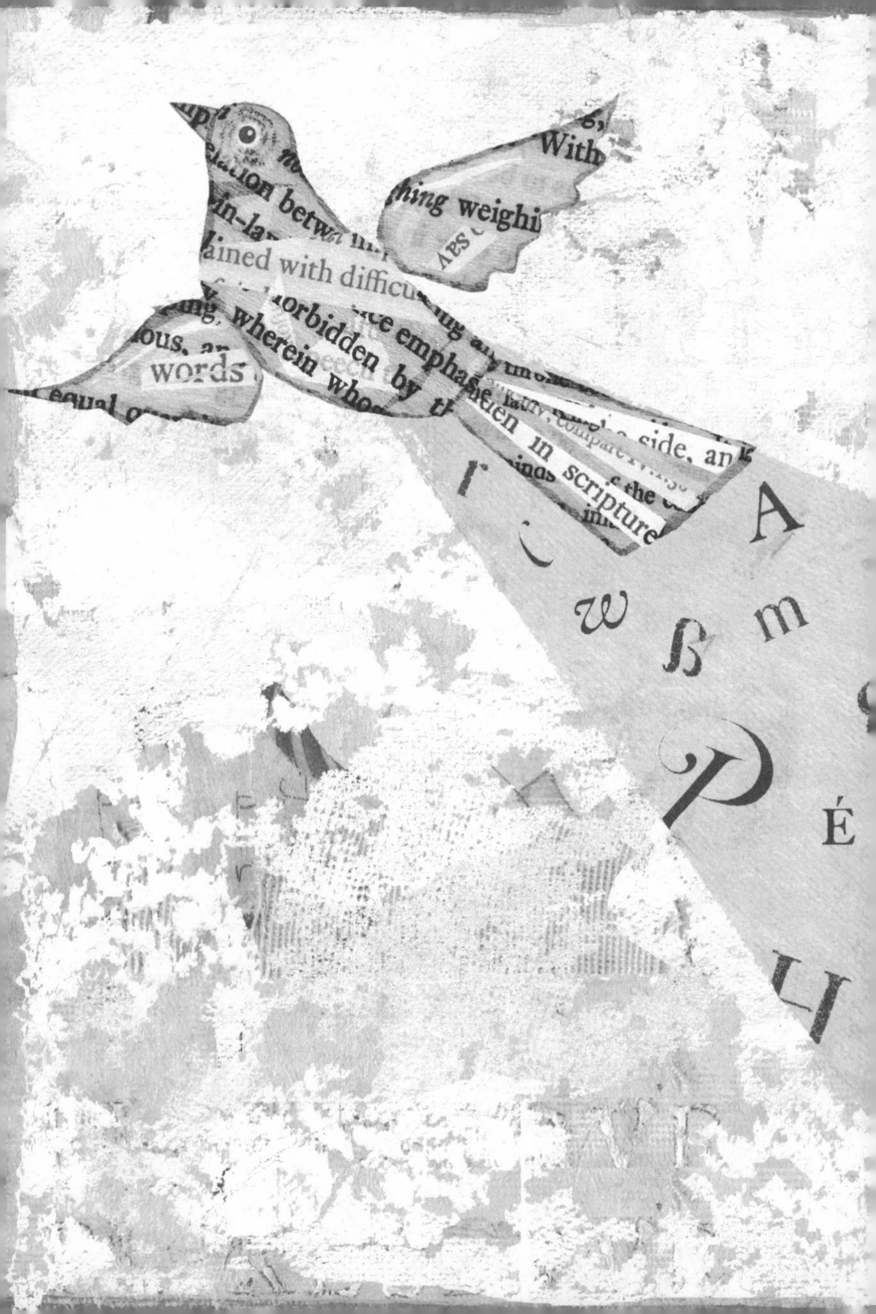

Part 3

New Pages: Finding Your Place in the World of Writing

Chapter 24

Fame and Fortune

FOR MANY WRITERS, THE DREAM OF PUBLISHING A BOOK IS AS far as they ever go. They nurse the dream, write some days, skip other days, and there it sits, this seemingly unattainable goal, like a mirage, a laurel wreath bestowed on only a lucky few.

How to be one of the chosen.

If you follow your heart, write only the pieces you alone can write, if you keep your mind open to learning, if you conquer lousy mental habits and self-defeating thinking, revise your work, join writing communities, and submit pieces to appropriate, well-researched markets, you will get published. Let me say this again. You will get published.

If you write every day, for a good while, maybe a year, or even three—if you put your time in the trenches, going to readings, studying your craft, working on other people's work, working on your own, and smartly sending it out, you will get published.

I know there are all these horror tales. Stories lost in the mail, unheralded geniuses all around us, their golden prose lost to time. Fabulous writers, forever unpublished.

You are not one of these people.

You write, page after page. If you write every day, you have *plenty* of writing. You work from a place of abundance. You know how to work, and working is 80 percent of knowing how to write.

Fame probably won't happen.

Fortune *definitely* probably won't happen.

But what can you expect after you win your first big or small award? What about when (and you will) you publish your first book, first poem, first article in a major periodical?

It will happen.

What's up with fame and fortune?

Not much.

A lot of beginning writers invest editors and publishers with power they don't have.

Most of publication and selection is subjective—no one is really in a position to say who deserves what. The person who suffered the most? For whom the writing was most difficult? The "best" writing—according to whom? Fame and fortune are random. There's not a board (thank goodness) doling out the prizes and book contracts to the deserving, in proper order. Publishers are generally people who love writing, who are really busy, trying to do good work.

The less time you spend trying to discern the mysterious ways of the publishing industry, the more time you have for your writing.

When I published my book, I was happy for one entire day, a twenty-four hour period. I called my parents. I called my ex-boyfriend (the box house guy). I called other friends. I told my boss and his boss. I hugged our departmental secretary, hard.

The next evening, I started feeling really bad, like I was getting the flu. Shaky and weak, my throat felt swollen, and my feet felt sweaty and numb.

What would my reviews be like? Who would read the book? How many copies would be published? What would my next book be? What if people hated the book? What would the cover be like? Who would write blurbs for the book?

There were so many weaknesses in the book (the dire lack of plot, for one).

What about the people from high school whose names I didn't change? Would that be slander or libel?

Waiting for my book to come out, I got really depressed, and it was even worse because this was my life's dream. If this wasn't going to make me happy, what was? The months waiting for the book to come out were horrible. I felt spoiled and obnoxious and bizarre—who isn't happy to be published?

I'd wanted to publish a book for my entire life. Since I was five years old. Twenty-seven years!

I thought, on some level, when I published my book that I would be a different person. Being a published author—it was supposed to open doors. I thought I would be a famous author. I thought there would be television coverage, interviews, great sales, travel all over the world. I thought I would be extremely popular. My dating life would surely improve. I would feel more confident, my skin pore size would decrease, my body would be stronger, my finances would be of the No More Worries variety.

Nothing changed, it just didn't.

I didn't morph into a different person.

I didn't even feel different or happier.

I got to become friends some great people at my publishing house, and I got to go on a small book tour, where very few people attended my readings and fewer bought books.

Sometimes I felt like the book was a passport—cocktail parties and bookstores and galas and panels and university reading series invitations—there's more of this if you are a published writer, less if you are not. With a book, *potentially* you can move around in more square footage. You still have to do the work, the research, the showing up, the daily writing, the going to the party. So, in that way, a book is not going to change anything, but it can offer (modest) potential for change. And that is a very great thing. I do not mean to diminish it in any one way.

But many writers nurture a dream that is false. You will get published. But it is unlikely that publication will solve any problems you have—blocks, money, habits, confidence, or writing ability.

It is very common for writers to be blocked after publishing the first book. "Sophomore slump" and "one hit wonder" aren't known syndromes for nothing. You can feel a pressure to fix all the problems of the first project *in the second book*. You start thinking. You are too aware of your audience. You aren't just you, unknown and unsung in your writing room, slogging away, you against the world. You feel like you should already know everything, so you may become less open to learning. Less beginner-ish. All these things make it hard to write, daily.

Fame and fortune must be fabulous. I love the idea of fame and fortune. When movie stars complain about how hard it is to grocery shop, I roll my eyes and sigh. Please. Give us a break. To be free from money worries, to be able to have flexibility in child care, parent care, real life care, to be respected and adored for what gives us such great pleasure—writing—it would be heavenly. I don't know that fame and fortune have a downside, exactly. Sloppy expectations, fantasy, and a lack of a commitment to doing the daily work—those have a downside.

Most writers I know, most who give readings on the national circuit, aren't well known. My students say, "I've never heard of that person." I know they haven't heard of me, or you, either.

This used to drive me nuts.

In our culture, writers aren't really famous. A few are, and more power to them, there must be some reason, some good reason, and I am happy for them. Most of us are known to a few other writers; maybe just in our region, or in our town, or on our street, we're "the writer."

Writers don't really get rich and famous. Ours is a completely other endeavor. It's pretty quiet, even for successful and super successful writers. Writing is one place where you can still be paid in *cents*. Even pork bellies are traded in dollars! We can still be paid 20¢ a word. Many magazines don't pay at all, they send "contributor copies." You send your work, they send you a few copies of the magazine. Some disreputable places even charge writers to publish their works. (Never send money to have someone publish you. Ever.)

Some writers, who work very hard, every day, make money off of their writing. Most, like painters and puppeteers and pianists, have other sources of income: lessons, shows, community performances. Most writers are less master and more jack-of-all-trades. It can be frustrating, but I think we like it that way. Most writers aren't terribly obnoxious or stuck-up or greedy for chic sunglasses and fancy cars. They like nice paper. Beautiful pencils. Maybe a particularly fine desk lamp or a gift certificate from a locally owned bookstore. I might be wrong, but I think most writers are going to do the work, anyway, for some other reason than fame or fortune. We are people of letters, as Janet Burroway says. We have to record what we see and what we know, in our towns and on our streets, in our families and in our daily lives. In this way, we are the opposite of fame and fortune.

Which isn't unfortunate.

If you are a writer, you are called to do it. You're going to keep doing it. Not for fame or fortune (but you will, of course, gratefully accept those should they come your way). Word by word, page by page, writing is what writers do. If you only influence and change one person (you can count yourself, like on your income taxes), you never know what the result might be, a year or one hundred years from now. You must write, and you need not always know what for.

Being a writer isn't going to make you rich and famous. It's like being a parent or foosball champion or a minister or a yogi or a med tech. It's what you do because it's cool to think and see and feel in this way, trying to communicate something vital about the human experience to other people. Writers are trying to complete the picture, contribute to the sum total of what is understood about us.

(Did you write today?)

ON YOUR PAGE: *Exercise 46*

You are on the television or radio interview show of your dreams. What are you going to talk about? How are you going to come across? What's your objective, being on this show? Write the scenario. Reflect on what needs to happen between now and then.

Chapter 25
Mentors

I HAVE FABULOUS INSTINCTS.

So do you.

In each of us, there is a wise self. Whenever you ask your-self, your wise self, a question, she or he will always give you the right answer. You just have to ask. Your mentor is right inside of you with fabulous advice, great contacts, and a deep enriched understanding of you and all your you-ness.

We aren't usually told this. We are often told we have to have a mentor. *Great writers have great mentors. It all depends on who you know. You have to have a mentor to make it in the writing world.* I hear this all the time. None of this is true.

Mentors are wonderful, and nothing replaces the advice and support of an accomplished person who is a number of steps ahead of you.

But as a beginner, there's a hitch. There's something else you need to be aware of, something more than "must have mentor."

I see my students take a kind of weird little path through this whole mentor conversation. They envision a wise bearded man, author of at least ten books and winner of sixteen teach-ing awards, who has them over to dinner at his house, where he reads their manuscripts instead of chewing his roast beef and then on the spot telephones his agent to say, "You have to sign Joey. He's going to be snapped up—get him now, the kid's brilliant, I'm telling you. Brilliant!"

If there isn't that in their lives, they feel they don't have a mentor. They feel they are failing at the writing thing. *Everyone says you have to have a mentor! Have to have a mentor! Can't get published without one!* Too many beginners falsely conclude they may as well give up.

The world doesn't owe us wise people. We owe the world the cultivation of our wisest self.

A better question than "How do I find a mentor?" is "How do I become mentor-able?"

You learn how to become a mentee. You don't demand mentors. There isn't some magical world out there where the secrets of the writing profession are being traded left and right with you deliberately excluded.

Once you are ready for a mentor, the mentor will appear. But it's going to take awhile. As a beginner, you are supposed to be working on your writing practice, showing up daily for work. What's the point of having a mentor if you aren't writing, and getting comfortable good mental habits?

The mentor isn't going to write for you.

Don't waste your mentor coupon.

Let's start with getting you ready. I see writers (at all stages of their careers) complaining about the lack of mentoring, their age, the isolated part of the country they live in, griping about everything that keeps them from being mentored into publication and fame, and right onto national television.

I would like to refocus all this energy on becoming mentor-able.

Mentor Lesson Number I: *Ya gotta go to the party.*

Mentors do not make house calls. Show up to everything. Book signings, library fundraisers, art openings, bookstore readings, visiting writers series, everything. Get to know local writers by attending their events. You'll drive how many hours to see a concert? Go see a writer.

Mentor Lesson Number 2: *Learn everything you can from books, journals, book reviews, and Web sites.*

Most of the questions beginners and even intermediate writers have are fully discussed in books. Let books mentor you to the place where you are mentor-ready. Save your mentor for the questions only another human can answer, in person. I bet you won't even know what those are for a while. Spend a few years reading, widely.

Mentor Lesson Number 3: *If you feel isolated, practice making contacts.*

Start writing letters to the authors you read. Follow up your bookstore and author event attendance with thank you notes. Go to conferences. Practice introducing yourself. I say practice, because you may feel very dweeb-like the first few times you do this. It's just practice, silly. It doesn't count yet. This person isn't going to be your mentor for real; you are still in the very beginning stages. Write letters to as many authors as you can, and don't ask for anything, just practice making brief, honest, positive remarks about their work, its impact on you, and so on. Simply send the letters to the publishers where your favorite people publish their books. Many writers will write you back. It doesn't matter, though, if they do or don't. You are readying yourself for your mentor.

In graduate school, for my master's and Ph.D., I had two great mentors. A mother, Janet Burroway, and a father,

Jerome Stern. It was wonderful to have two mentors; I was doubly blessed, and I didn't know at the time how valuable this attention and support and counsel was, or how rare. However, I saved them up. I used my advisors' time carefully. I knew they were the best people for me to work with, but I didn't go to them right away. It was *two years* before I showed my face in their offices, asking my questions. I spent a lot of time preparing to be mentored by these two great people.

First, I took every writing class I could. I did all the extra credit and all the recommended readings. I went to every party to which I was invited, and while it made me nervous as hell—I *hated* parties—I made myself go. When writers came to town, I read their books. During the question and answer sessions, I always *forced* myself to ask one question. I felt like a complete idiot, but somewhere, deep down inside, I knew I needed to learn how to do this, Real Life.

I wanted not to waste a single moment of my mentors' time. I wanted the marrow, the very heart of what they had to offer me. So, I practiced on other professors, the weaker teachers, first. I was weak, they were weak—it was a good match. I practiced on visitors, and other graduate students, asking questions, launching large convoluted goofy theories about art and tension and trauma. I felt like I was constantly grooming myself to be worthy of the best advice.

I wrote a bunch of bad stories, took lots of mediocre classes, and developed friendships with (gotta go to the party) the students in the wise teachers' classes. I went out with them, the big kids, the publishing students, after their workshops, to the local pub where they would hang out and talk about everyone and their writing. Hanging out with the wise ones, I sat at those tables in the Grand Finale and took actual notes, wrote things down *at the table*. Buffalo wings were big in those days and my notes from those two years are stained with orange wing grease.

I learned about fiction, workshop politics, how to work in a group, what didn't fly, what people were like. I learned how not to embarrass myself, what not to say, what not to do. I learned to contribute to a conversation but not dominate. I learned you have to say something if you want to keep your seat at the table. I learned how to become more serious and lighter at the same time.

I read every single book and magazine on creative writing I could get my hands on. I really read a lot.

Then, finally, I felt ready.

I took a class with Janet. She would be my mother. I wrote down everything she said in class. I'd already read all her books. I thought all the students would be doing this—I still saw myself as the dumb girl in a bathing suit from Orlando, no real brainpower, not a good fit for graduate school. I asked her questions about poetry, about plot, about publication, and she gave long, smart, and wonderful answers. I wrote down everything she said. Often she said, "The best solution is going to be found in the next draft you do."

And I worked. I wrote.

Sometimes you might get lucky and have a mentor who truly shapes your whole career, your whole life. Some people live in New York with wealthy literary uncles. John Updike is sent to your eighth grade English class to talk; "they" publish your first story in *The New Yorker*; some people have that.

But what I have found is that you earn your mentors. Most

all the information you need is at your fingertips, and you do have to show up for the party—prepared. Your best mentors? Good library skills. Good social skills.

You aren't passive. You have a great brain and a wise self. Next time you are pining for a mentor, ask yourself the question. You might be surprised at the answer.

On the other hand, if the reason you want a mentor is because you want to be regally cheered up and reassured, you need a therapist, or a friend, or a juicy novel. Not some wise ancient powerbroker of literature ensconced in a high rise in New York. Pay attention to what you are looking for.

My other mentor, Jerry, would become my surrogate father. He taught me to not complain—that complaining keeps you back, tied down. He taught me how to layer my writing, and how to keep my edge without confusing or troubling the reader. He taught me that I am writing for the reader, not to express my own personal melodrama. He said: "Develop your subjects." The best piece of advice I ever got in my whole life. So, I'll say it again: *Develop your subjects.*

Develop your subjects means instead of stewing, whining, freaking out, getting upset, obsessing on your terrible child-hood, or lying about like a sludge-pile, you have to learn new stuff. Learn interesting things. Study the rare ghost orchid. Become one of six people in the world who knows about dia-betes in trees. Immerse yourself in semiotics or the history of radio. Indulge a time-consuming and difficult hobby. You have to be out in the world in a complex, engaged way in order to grow as a person, and to grow as a writer, you must grow, wisely, as a person. Take flamenco, tae kwon do, or tap. Learn how to heal with ancient herbs, learn Hebrew, or do greyhound rescue. You need to meet interesting people in order to be a writer. You need to develop some subjects, and you will always need to be doing this, the rest of your life.

Freud says it. Nietszche says it. Jesus says it. You have two things in your life: work and love.

Thread your work with interesting strands, ones that insist you apprehend new knowledge.

Now that's a mentor!

During this period of being a mentee to Jerry and Janet, I was having a really hard time. My parents were very advanced in their needs. I was being stalked by an escaped mental patient. I was running the Visiting Writers Series with Jerry, and it was very intimidating, talking to famous people and making sure they had things the way they needed them to be.

I was crying a lot and exhausted (remember, I was taking all those extra classes and reading all that extra reading), and this made me nervous. I didn't want to scare people away. I wanted friends. Sometimes the crying came out of nowhere. I kind of liked being so dramatic and tormented—I was reading a lot of Henry Miller, Sylvia Plath, Anaïs Nin, and watching a lot of Betty Boop. I felt like I fit in with wonderfully depressed icons of despair. I felt like I was one step away from the apartment in Paris, the string of handsome lovers, tango lessons.

One final, vital thing you have to do if you want mentors: You have to listen and then do what they say. A lot of the people I hear complaining about their lack of mentoring don't take the advice they *do* get!

You must take advantage of all the ways you're already being mentored before anyone is going to find you an appealing project to take on. Mentoring is all around you. Get on it.

I know a lot of people who complain. I used to wonder about this a lot. I knew I had been mentored, beautifully. But when I look back on it, I see that I really did my part, too. I was a great mentee. Some people just like to say they want a mentor. They don't seem to really want to know more information. They need an excuse as to why they aren't writing.

Mentors are made by mentees.

Remember, you aren't entitled to a mentor. You have to give the one inside of you a lot of training. You might get another one. You might not. You know the old saw: The teacher appears when the student is ready. Have you learned everything you can on your own? Are you ready?

It's like love. Needy people don't find good love. Happy, independent, hardworking people attract fabulous partners.

Too much need quashes love. Passivity quashes mentoring.

ON YOUR PAGE: *Exercise 47*

Make a list of all the people who give you information. It doesn't have to relate to writing—just list the people in your life you go to for information. List ten people, at least.

One good way to attract a new mentor into your world is to pay homage to those you already have.

Can you write them a note, buy them a book, or in some other way thank them for giving you information? Being a good recipient of information will attract more wisdom to your life!

ON YOUR PAGE: *Exercise 48*

If you had a mentor, a wise accomplished writer who could come over tonight after dinner, what would you ask this person? Write down all your questions. Go wild, don't consider any question too small or too big.

Put the list away for one week. This gives your internal mentor, that wise person I promise lives within you, a chance to work on the questions during his/her free time. In a week, go over your list. Read the questions out loud. Can you answer any of them? Are you surprised? This is a powerful exercise for learning to trust your own inner compass.

Alternatively, do this with a friend. Trade lists, and answer each other's questions—as many as you can.

ON YOUR PAGE: *Exercise 49*

Develop your subjects. Make a list—ten to twenty items—of subjects you would love to pursue. The stock market? Dreamweaver? This nature of myths and rituals? Con artistry, dominoes, Scrabble? Chess online? The history of movie criticism? Squirrels? What do you want to know more about? It's kind of like you are designing a curriculum tailored just to you, your dream semester, your perfect courseload.

Circle the most appealing item on your list. At the library (you are making regular trips, right? Don't you have some Writer's Market assignments to get caught up on?), check out a book or a video on this topic, and begin learning.

You don't need to actively write about this new subject. You don't have to study floral arranging or Reiki just because you want to insert it into your novel or essays or a poem. Learn for the sake of learning. The exact right stuff will sift down into your work—the less intentional you are, the better. Don't force it. Read like a kid—for the pure pleasure of learning.

Chapter 26

Rejection, Bliss, Speeding Tickets

DRIVING HOME FROM ALBANY LAST WEEKEND, I SAW IT again. The strained, grumpy face of a person sitting in his car, pulled over on the side of the road, the candy-colored flashers of the police car flinging accusatory light. He was really mad.

Like you, I have some talents, some things I am just blessed to be really, really good at. Being pulled over is one of them. I am, for some unknown reason, able to remain cheery.

Last time I was pulled over was on Christmas Eve. I was running late and lonesome and speeding down 26th Street.

"Do you know how fast you were going?" the officer said.

"I am sorry. I think I was doing maybe forty miles an hour. This is a twenty-five, I bet. I'm really sorry. I am at fault here."

I always own up to my speed. I thank the cop for doing her job. I enjoy freaking people out.

I was speeding. I got caught.

Why would I get mad?

Why is *everyone* who is pulled over surly and surprised and pissed off? Some of these people had to be speeding, right? I mean, it's not just bad luck coming down from the heavens upon you.

My job is to get where I'm going at the pace I think I need to be going; the cop's job is to say, "Hey, not so fast."

The rules are clear; I know I have to pay to play. I see my speeding tickets as a kind of tax—the fast tax. You pay it, and you move on. (And, yes, my cheer and authentic friendliness, my ready admission of how fast I was really going are so refreshing to the officer, I have had reduced and excused fines.)

When I'm genuinely in the wrong, it's not that hard for me to admit it. This is a gift I was born with. Maybe you have gorgeous hair, perfect eyebrows, money, or a beautiful voice, or maybe you're great with color or people. My gift is "wrong and admitting it."

Mine is an odd blessing, but one that has been extremely useful in my writing life.

Most people hate rejection. It's awfully easy to personalize it. We see the officer as singling us out and tormenting us. We see our trouble as unfair, which is so dumb. As though somehow we are more special than other people. Exempt. Chosen.

Please.

Get pulled over, pay your taxes. When you lock your keys in your car, when you forget to pay your credit card bill and you get late fees, just smile, and pay. Thank the person on the other end, don't call and whine and create a whole personal defense when you are wrong! Realize, if you can—and I know this is annoying as a personality trait—that this is part of the deal. There's this account, this universal fund, and we all have to pay into it. We all have to lose our wallets, get our purses stolen, misplace our keys, and have our cars break down— somewhere, someone has to do this, or the world would stop or something. When it's your turn, just go with it. It's a tax. It's unimportant. Simply pay, and continue your happy play.

You can learn to embrace rejection. To welcome it, to not be ruffled, offended, or affected by it. You might not want to develop this trait—we'll call this chapter "optional." People who are cheerful in the midst of trouble are irritating to be around. I try to keep this aspect of my life to myself, but I do try to tell my students that rejection isn't really meaningful or interesting. It certainly has nothing to do with you, yourself, or your writing life. All that matters is that you show up and do it every day. If you are rejecting *yourself*, well, that is another story (and the subject of many chapters in this book).

What a relief it is to say, "I am so wrong. I am wrong." "I left the coffee maker on. It was me." "I didn't really come by your office, I just thought about it." "I was going sixty in a forty-five, maybe even seventy."

You will be so much more fluid and less brittle when you practice making friends with error. The honesty gives you more space in which to work.

For writers, rejection is a way of life. It helps to breathe in rejection, get closer to it. Don't tense up. Maybe if you put rejection in another light, if you surprise rejection, you will be amazed at the energy you have freed up. Can you tell yourself a different story about rejection?

There's lots of advice about how to handle rejection: Ignore it, learn from it, don't revise until sixteen places have rejected your poem, revise after ten rejections, save all your rejection slips, get rid of all your rejection slips—it goes on and on. None of that is actually really useful, is it?

Another friend of mine, Roberta, says you have to realize editors select works—they don't actively pick you out and say "Not you, missy."

"It's a selection process, not a rejection process,"
Roberta keeps saying. She edits a magazine, so to her, I
guess, it is. Doesn't feel like selection though when you get
an e-mail from an intern saying your work isn't "right" for
Fancy Schmancy Pants Today.

I send my work out to magazines and publishers and agents
(of course in the hope it will be published and adored and
make me millions). I send my work out, a lot. I also write every
day, and revise a lot. I stay really busy at it (no errands!). And,
when the rejection slips and letters and postcards come back, I
don't give them more thought than you would any piece of
business mail. These notes are like "hellos" from very, very
distant relatives. I pick up my rejection note, squint, try to
make out something of interest, and then—can you guess?—I
go back up to my writing room and work.

Now, this is a very drama-free way of handling life and not
really interesting. It's way more exciting to feel pain and horror, to wonder deeply and endlessly about the worth of your
piece, the intelligence of editors, why so many bad books are
published—that whole sack of cats. You can call up all your
friends and have that same conversation.

Or, you can pay absolutely no attention to any of that at all.

Because it doesn't matter one whit.

The relationship of who writes great stuff, who gets published, and who gets rejected actually doesn't make any sense.
Even if it does make sense to someone smarter than I am, it's
not our job to figure out stuff like that. We are the writers!
We're supposed to be writing. Other people (Lawyers?
Editors? Paper companies? Small children? People with way
more time on their hands than we have on ours?) can worry

about who is published and why. While it's very good and smart to study your market, and to have your work read by your very smartest, most savvy friends, attaching significance to a rejection is like believing in Santa. There is no Santa. There is no board up in the heavens arbitrating great literature. There is no god who makes sure the diligent fabulous hard-working writers get published and the fakers suffer.

It doesn't work that way.

It can't. The publishing world is a bunch of people, with aging parents and children, and loud neighbors, locking their keys in their car, losing their wallets, renovating their kitchens, and getting the flu. They do their best. You don't worry about it, and keep writing each day.

I want you to be honest with yourself about what is really going on when you send out a piece of work, and it comes back with a little preprinted note: *Sorry, this isn't right for us.* Or, when you take a piece of writing to your writing group and they say, *Honey, we're sorry, but this just isn't your best work—maybe you should move on to the next poem?*

A person is reacting to your work. Maybe for good reasons, with good intentions. Maybe she doesn't know anything. We give our rejectors all this power that they don't deserve—it's kind of insane.

Your confidence as a writer is going to come from the strength you get in establishing a regular writing practice. Something you can count on. While publication is very juicy and sexy and delicious, it doesn't change the fact that you will have to go write. You need to focus on that.

I don't think about it much anymore, but when I began writing, I was very aware that my chosen occupation featured rejection as a way of life. Since I was a beginner, I counted on the fact that my work would probably be rejected until I learned how to write better. I sent my work to magazines and contests, though, hoping it would be published and win prizes, but at heart, fairly certain that I still had a lot to learn about how to write. My work was rejected. Hundreds and hundreds of times. I'd read that "real" writers sometimes papered their walls with their rejection slips; for a while I thought that was a good idea. I taped hundreds of little pink and blue and white "sorry, not for us" slips of paper on the pine paneling in the kitchen of the house I shared with my boyfriend. It felt like earning brownie badges. Guests were impressed that I'd sent out that much stuff. They were impressed I stuck with it. My parents thought I should take a hint. I thought I was just beginning, why would I get published anyway?

I still feel that way. I'm beginning. Publication, when it comes, is a thrill, a treat. It's not why I write. And if you're going to publish, you're going to get rejected a whole lot more than you're going to get accepted. You can set this up to be stressful, or you can lighten up, and keep your eye on the road—the writing.

Here's how I do it. I do a big submission fest, twice a year. Over winter break, and at the end of summer, I send out everything I have that's good. Everything I've worked on, hard. These are pieces I have copied over and over. My average number of drafts for a piece I am going to send out is seventeen. I send out everything. I scrape the bottom of the barrel. I work on pieces—I feel like I'm in the theatre and I'm getting a bunch of kids ready for the seasonal revue. None of them can sing at first, but some are kind of cute and a few can dance.

So, everybody goes out. Successful submitting requires only two skills—that you read magazines like the ones you want to get into, subscribing to as many as your funding will allow. And, the secretary who lives inside you has to go to the office supply store and photocopy and organize all these pieces of paper.

My inner secretary tracks all this out on a spreadsheet. It takes an average of ten tries for a story to be published. Ten submissions. So, you see, I'm just twiddling my thumbs on submissions one through nine—it's not a big deal. The submitting is part of the stripes the story has to earn. It has to go out there! Mix it up! Run with the big dogs. It has nothing to do with me. People publish work. You and I are writers. Sometimes paths will cross, and that's a good thing.

Publishing isn't personal.

Publishing doesn't change your life or make it easier to write.

So, when a story or poem or essay comes back to me, which, obviously, it does rather frequently (about four months after submission, on average), several things occur. First of all, I am eager for the story to come back so I can send it out again and get to my ten times. Second, I feel like a real writer. Third, I enjoy even more (it's akin to watching *Survivor*) the magazines' next issues—who did they choose? Often, writers I like a lot. Fourth, after enough time passes, I begin to see the piece differently. (If you are doing the math, you can see the whole endeavor takes years, potentially, for just one piece—again, this is why we are writing every day.) And revision isn't a chore, I'm excited to have a new way into the piece.

My first book was rejected seventeen times. While at the end of that run, I was getting a little … impatient, I just didn't worry that much—I enjoyed the process. I really loved it. I felt as I do when I freak out a cop, that I was paying smart attention to the right things in the writing world, chiefly, writing and submitting my work.

I can even say I like rejection. It gives me an important window of time with my work. While the pieces are out there, circulating through the hands of busy, hopefully wise reader-editors, my words are in limbo. I think something important happens between you and the piece you've sent out, and you both come back together, smarter. I have a photographer friend, Diane, who puts her prints in a box and leaves them there for two months to "cure." Like whiskey or bacon, the prints, she believes, grow richer and deeper and more complex when left alone for a while. Or, what you know about the piece you've written grows more funky and complex and interesting. I saw Diane's big flat curing box, and understood immediately that this was what happened when I sent a story into the mail. It's a way of getting distance, literally, on your work. The piece goes away, far, far away—into the darkness in Diane's case, to Topeka or Boston or Stillwater in my case—and when you peek at it again, open that envelope of surprise, there you have it: The story is a bit of a stranger to you. It's not so much your heart walking around outside your body. It's something you can work with. It comes back to you, after being cured, more eatable, more tasty, and also, most importantly, more change-able. *It* hasn't changed, but you have, in some tiny way, and sometimes there's an alchemy there that wasn't possible before.

So the pieces come back. One after the other. Slowly, but surely. And I either work on the piece a little more—now that I have been away from it for four months (the least amount of time an editor might take in reviewing your article or story), I can see typos, weak writing, flat scenes, cheese, complexities I hadn't known to develop before. I'm a little less in love with the piece, and also, so happy to see it again. Or, I send the piece back out. Right back out. I have a rule: No rejected work spends the night in my house. (This rule works well in dating as well as in creative writing.)

If the piece has been circulating for two years (not unusual), I might take another look at it, see how the curing process is treating the little wayward story. One of my most successful stories—a story my writing group hated, and my mother found so shocking she literally did not *speak* to me for months, a story rejected by *thirty* places—eventually won three major prizes. I left it alone. I kept sending it out. It's in a famous anthology. I still get occasional letters about that story.

How do you know which to do—do you keep sending or keep revising? Forget the whole thing? I advise you to spend no more than one-tenth of your total writing time working (even thinking!) about these problems. They aren't important. What's important is that you show up to your writing appointments and write. But submitting work is a fun hobby—just keep it that way. Don't let submitting your work and waiting for rejections dominate or drive your writing life. It's a tiny thing, and you do it on the side. Wholly on the side. You shouldn't talk about this aspect of your writing life. Don't complain, don't fret, don't try to predict, or suspect a conspiracy. Editors take a long time. That's part of the deal.

If a piece is rejected ten times, I consider revising.

Sometimes I don't revise the piece at all, ever. Sometimes I revise while the piece is making its rounds. There's no reason to get rigid, or try to read some tea leaves that don't even exist.

If I feel like revising, I do. If I don't, I don't. Remember, this is supposed to be fun. This is your writing life *hobby*. Too many writers get very weird about all this. You don't have to.

One tip: If your piece keeps coming back, and you hear yourself saying, *I know this is good, why won't they publish it?* you probably need to revise more.

You have to grin at the sending out process. You have to mail with a light touch. You have to realize that if you are speeding, you are fair game for getting caught. If you are rushing through your writing life, skipping your own writing practice sessions, running red lights, not reading, not taking yourself and your commitment seriously, you are going to get pulled over. Stopped short.

If you are a beginning writer, expect to be rejected—go ahead and put yourself in the position of being rejected one hundred times! Make it a game, make it a goal. Don't ever complain about your work being rejected or how slow the writing world is; you already know that's part of what you signed up for. Enjoy this ride. Focus on how lucky you are to have a car, so to speak, to get to drive at all. At first, your job is to learn how to be rejected with grace and style, and, if you can muster it, even enthusiasm.

Get real. Get rejected.

Find opportunities to improve your work. That's how you want to spend your time. Resist the crack cocaine of the writer's complaints and don't whine about how long editors take, or how quixotic the whole thing is. Don't ever say, "What do they *want*?" They want simple, clear, pure, true pieces— smart and from your heart. They want clean, proofread, beautiful writing. Polished, honed, and not too long. Something with some layers, something that took time to make. That's all anyone wants. What we want in a nice meal is the same thing we want in art or a great conversation. Something with layers, something that took some time.

Write more pieces so more editors have more work by you on their desks, or, more likely, in the backseat of their cars, next to mashed Cheerios and babyseats and umbrellas and thousands of other stories, waiting to be read by the editors speeding along through their own busy, busy lives.

It's not about you, so much.

It's about your writing practice.

Write more. Get rejected more.

Fool the story into becoming its best possible self—by submitting it, by curing it, by sending it to school, by ignoring it, by lavishing attention and newfound writing insights on it.

Make allowances for speed, and for slowness. You're going to have to get a new attitude—and not your junior high prom attitude—about rejection. I'm not saying this is easy, but I am telling you that it can be, almost, fun. Submitting work takes a really long time. It takes a lot of your precious writing time to get all the envelopes and paperwork and record-keeping in order. It takes editors a lot of time to read the hundreds (true) of submissions they get every week.

Write more.

Think about it less.

Next time you get pulled over, grin.

ON YOUR PAGE: *Exercise 50*

After you have written for five days straight, you deserve a marketing day. Author Carolyn See always does her writing-life business at the beginning of the week; she calls them Marketing Mondays. For your first marketing day, go to the library and look at the new edition of *Writer's Market*. Some libraries keep it in Reference. Some keep it on the shelves with writing guide books, like this one. Editions of *Writer's Market* are easy to find because they are huge tomes. (The Web site for *Writer's Market* is www.writersmarket.com.)

Read the front chapters, short chapters by writers and editors loaded with good practical tips on how you get published.

Then, go to the back of the book. See the sections in the part called Subject Index? This is a good place to start. When you find a section that seems to fit your bent as a writer, start writing down magazine titles and page numbers. You're on your way!

Maybe you are "health/medicine" or "short story collections" or "multicultural." Maybe your book of stories about doctors in Haiti places you in all three categories—wonderful. There are probably at least a few sections that fit you and your work, or your writing to come.

Make a list of forty places you could send your work to.

Then, the legwork. And this is vitally important. (This might take more than one Marketing Monday session.) Let's say you fish, and you also have written some poems about giant saltwater fish, humorous little poems. You read the entries for the places on your list. You find *Salt Water Sportsman Magazine*.

Read the entry again. Check out the little codes, telling you how hard it is to get into the magazine if you have never published before, and how much they pay new writers, if anything at all.

Remember, you aren't in this for the money, but for the experience of being rejected—you need those one hundred rejections so you can get to Intermediate in your writing life! The blurb below the magazine title gives you vitally important information about when you can submit, what the editors are looking for, what they will and won't read. Many of the entries have fabulous "Tips" sections. Read all of this.

Put your list in priority order, so you could send a piece to your first choice place, then have thirty-nine more chances.

ON YOUR PAGE: *Exercise 51*

While you are at the library, there's one more thing you have to do. And you can do both of these exercises a little bit at a time.

You need to check out the forty different magazines, take them home, and read them. You can't skip this step! You can't submit "blind"—meaning, you must know the pages, intimately, that will one day carry your words on them. You have to know your market. You have to read, and keep reading, funky, off-beat, small magazines. People who publish know their competition. They know the editors' tastes at each place they submit.

If your library doesn't carry *Porthole Cruise Magazine* then you can usually write for two things (and you must): (1) that magazine's "writer's guidelines," and (2) a sample copy, usually only a couple of dollars. The writer's guidelines will always be free (you usually have to include a self-addressed, stamped envelope, called a SASE). More and more, these guidelines are appearing on magazine Web sites.

Chapter 27
False Modesty

IS THERE ANY OTHER KIND OF MODESTY?

This is one of those words. *Modest*. I hate it.

I grew up in a home where one of the values was, purportedly, modesty. Don't brag on yourself. Don't be self-centered.

Sadly, most of us who are raised with these values also get their unwanted cousins as add-ons:

Don't brag, which means *don't notice or value your own accomplishments*.

Don't be self-centered, which essentially plays out as *don't be self-aware*.

Don't be self-indulgent, which means what, *cultivate unhappiness*?

Ugh.

I think modesty might be about the most self-focused, unwise, *false* thing you can sell yourself. I deeply believe, trust, know that the act of being comfortable with yourself, is more "modest" and true than pretending otherwise. "Modesty" seems so manipulative and needy.

It takes a brave leap to say, "Yes, I just wrote a really kick-ass poem. It's good. I'm good!"

People have criticized those of us with verve, a strong color-ful life force, abundant strength, those of us who find comfort in our energy and power. I have heard people say in a thousand ways, "You are taking up too much room, you are too big." One person wrote me and said, "Who do you think you are?" Another person, a friend said to me, "Creative writing is so self-indulgent." Friends!

It surprises me. Then it stings a little. Then I remember the point: I am trying to laugh louder and more often, to celebrate my accomplishments instead of grooving on my failures and whining. I'm trying to enjoy gaining weight, frolicking. I'm trying to spend more time writing more reams of words, many of which will be in such a good order, they'll hurt.

When people want me to be smaller, I no longer take it personally. This is the great growth mark of my early thirties. Now, I realize my critics are afraid of their own size or talents. It is scary to know you are good. It is unsettling to have happy, confident folks around when you feel less than good.

It's flying without a net. You might be wrong!

Modesty is a false crutch. It's a way of saying "poor me."

As I am more comfortable being good, I'm more comfortable with my many, many screwups. It's easy to say now, "Oh, I was really stupid! Thank you for noticing that."

In yoga, whenever you do a move, you always do what is called a "counterpose." If you lean forward for a while, then you do a back bend. You are always balancing yourself. Hear this: We spend most of our time in our heads, beating ourselves up, and criticizing everybody else along the way. Much of our internal dialogue is saying "Why the heck did you do that, you idiot?"

If you spend your morning writing, do you also say to yourself, "What are you thinking? You have children! People are starving! You could have mowed the yard! Look at the mess!"

Do you say, "This is terrible writing, why are you doing this?" Do you say to yourself, one hundred times a day in a hundred different ways, "Who do you think you are?"

I thought so.

This is not good. Other people are already telling you this, now you are in on the hijinks too? Not good!

So, what is it, exactly, modesty? It's a terrible fake-out, and we must banish it from our lives.

Recently, I was at a conference of writers, editors, agents, and writing teachers. Lots of the attendees are published, working writers. I gave a reading at this conference, and later that night when I was asked how my reading went (I read right after famous poet Donald Hall), I said I felt like I had done a really good job. "It was good. I did well. I like to read," I said.

My interlocutor and his friend both laughed. The friend said, "Oh, and you are modest, too?"

I cringed. I really hate these moments. Am I supposed to say I did a terrible job? That I wasn't sure?

The modesty game is silly.

I was not bragging. I wasn't saying I did well when I didn't. I wasn't saying I was the greatest living thing in the universe. I had enjoyed myself, given a good reading (for which I pre-pared at great length). I did a good job—that was the whole point. I wanted to do a good job.

At the party, I wafted away from the two who wanted me to be smaller. I looked for a happy person, taking up a lot of room. An immodest person. A person who knew good from false, and modest from real.

I think this weird state called "modesty" is always false. Sometimes the "modest" person is really saying, *Tell me more, say it again.* You know those conversations, the insecure meeting the false:

"You were great!"

"No I wasn't!"

"Yes you were!"

"No I wasn't!"

"You were!"

I hate those conversations.

When I find myself singing false notes like that, high, breathy, airy, baseless notes, I know I'm not being the person I was meant to be.

I started learning this lesson from Mary Jane, a fellow poet/fiction writer/Betty Boop aficionado I knew in graduate school.

"Your story was great," she said after a workshop. We were in the dusty tile women's room on the third floor of Williams. She was putting on red lipstick.

"No, it wasn't," I said. I remember my hands bursting into sweat, my feet slipping in my sandals. My basic fear response—leak lots of water.

"You know, Heather," Mary Jane said to me. "When I get a compliment, I try to accept it. It's hard, but I'm practicing. If your story was good, and you know it was good, you can say *thanks*. It's okay to do that. To accept a compliment. When you deserve it. Man, life is hard enough, you know? We don't have to reject the good stuff on top of everything else."

Mary Jane flounced out of the bathroom. I looked in the mirror, which tilted toward the floor, so if you were in a wheelchair, you could also see yourself. I leaned down, and looked at my face.

Was my story good?

I liked it.

"Thanks," I mouthed to my little round sweaty face. I started practicing in the little slanty mirror. "Thanks," I said. I grinned. It felt funny, and wonderful. I have been practicing ever since.

What if you can't tell if your work is good or not? (Often, you can't.) What if it is sort of good and sort of not good? What if you could make it so much better? Isn't accepting compliments at the wrong juncture worse than false modesty? Aren't you in danger of becoming an ego queen, a person with a false sense of self?

Aren't you going to be self-indulgent, a fool if you go around thinking you are the hottest little thing?

In a word, no.

That's not going to happen.

At that conference I attended, there were other incidences of the false modesty syndrome. There were so many! A number of people said to me, "Will you send us your work?" "Will you read at our school?" "Where can I buy your book?"

And an equal number of people said to me, one way or another, "Who do you think you are?"

I heard my mother's voice echoing, *Who do you think you are?*

I also heard Nell Haywood, in seventh grade, saying under her breath as I walked by, "She thinks she's so hot!"

Which I assure you, I did not.

Find ways to develop self-awareness so you know what you do well—ice cakes, train dogs, cry, nurture parents, fall in love, grow climbing roses—you do a thousand things brilliantly, and if you don't know what they are, you aren't going to be able to become a true evaluator of your own work or other people's. You are going to be one of those people who give false compliments (flattery) and don't know how to take the truth.

Sometimes you're good.

Sometimes you suck.

You triumph. You err.

Sometimes you are brilliant. And sometimes, in the exact same moment, you are wretched and foolish.

You can practice being comfortable with the differences.

You can know.

This is not cocky or sassy or stuck-on-self. Let's call it "awake."

At my book signing that day, people lined up. They said "This book is so good." I said "Thanks! I am so happy you like it. Do you write too?"

I was happy and joyous and free, signing my name, knowing what is good.

ON YOUR PAGE: *Exercise 52*

The De-modest-ification Process begins today:

a. *Make a list of everything this week you did that was really rather brilliant. Think tiny:*

> Ordered white andouille sausages (tried something new)
> Went to bed early, woke up beautiful and rested
> Bought Slinkies to give to kids next door

b. *Now, writing fast and not thinking even a little bit, make a list of ten titles for your next ten books—just make 'em up:*

> Write for You: a self-help yoga writer book/autobiography

Girls From Other Planets: *a book of poetry*
Blossom and Kate: *a young adult novel*
Deans and Cannibals: *essays on academia*
The Plain and Simple Truth: *a novel*
Black River: *a novel set in an arts high school with sex and murder*
The Labyrinth and the Last Supper: *essays on religion*
Little Lips: *poems*
Cubby in Review: *a series of picture books*

c. *You are a fancy, well-paid, stunningly beautiful and beautifully dressed New York book reviewer. You only review things you adore. You want everyone else to read the books you love. (You are not you, but this whole other person, the generous wildly-in-love-with-your-work book reviewer.) Get in this mood.*

d. *Write a review of you, of your day, today. Use the rhetorical mode of the review. "She opens the day with a most enchanting bath, and you dear reader are hooked from the first paragraph. After buying Slinkies for neighborhood urchins, this amazing creature takes you on a ..." Have at it—you want the world to take you home, and share you with all its friends.*

e. *Write a review of one of your unborn books. Praise it to the skies. And, without telling lies. Be your most accurate and most honest praising self.*

Chapter 28
Workshops

IF, AFTER A YEAR OR A MONTH OR A DECADE YOU ARE
writing daily and wondering what you don't know about
writing, it might be time to add a tool to your writing life
toolkit. Writing workshops can be wonderful.

It was a hideous experience, my first fiction writing
workshop.

For class, I had written a story about a sixteen-year-old girl
who meets a preacher, a priest, actually, on the dock of a mysterious lake for a talk about redemption.

The class hated the story. "The writer seems like she just
read *Lolita*," Jeff said. I was in love with Jeff. I had just read
Lolita. I thought it a bit rude of him to bring up the similari-
ties (of which there were many of the most superficial nature).
Somehow, in my mind, I had decided my prose would be so
brilliant, *no one would notice I had just read Lolita*. I am not sure
how I duped myself into this belief.

But, after you write your first story and take it to workshop,
you can do pretty amazing things in the department of self-
deception.

It was very hard to have my story torn to shreds. I was physically sick to my stomach—I mean to say I puked—that night. It
was awful. I was so embarrassed. I felt stripped to the marrow
of my poor dumb bones. I cried and carried on in my

boyfriend's arms. "I am dirt. I am shit—how could you let me turn in such hideous shit as *fiction*?" I cried.

He said it was a fine story, and there were some really nice descriptions, like of the snakes. And the flashback had potential, he said.

Actual puke-taste was still in my mouth. But I smiled a little. "The flashback?" I said. "Let's hear more about that."

Three weeks later, I subjected myself to the bizarre, painful flagellation again. This time my story was about a library street party. A kind of fair, with clowns and candy, that a library sponsored. (I know, I know now.) Pam said my piece was interesting, but you couldn't tell what was going on. (This was true.) Claudia said I should stop writing about psychotic mothers. (This was not true.) Again, that night, I wept in my boyfriend's arms. How could I be such a bad writer?

"There were good parts. I like that whole thing about the scabs," he said, very kindly. He made a fire in our fireplace and we snuggled, and he read poems to me by Tomas Transtromer. It was very nice, really.

"Were there any other parts you liked?" I said. "Let's find more."

My first workshops were horrible experiences. Sharing work with my peers was like jumping off the high dive and into poisonous nuclear-toxic concrete. It was the hardest thing I have ever done. The stories were so awful and some of the comments were mean, true, honest, not-helpful. Somehow, though, I knew that I would get better if I kept writing, and bringing my terrible flawed creations, my work, to these mangy, scrabbly groups, filled with other bad writers, just like me.

Already, I had done more as a writer than my parents had done. I'd shown my work to a jury of my peers, and, I'd survived.

And it worked.

It really did. My writing got better. After my third workshop, I could tell. I was starting to make more interesting mistakes.

There's a lot of strange mystery about workshops. Some people say, "Oh workshops. Everyone learns to write the same." This, in my experience, is decidedly untrue. Other people say workshops damage you, they're nothing but personality contests. Still others bash the workshop method, saying it's competitive and damaging and unnecessary.

But I believe in workshops. I believe workshops work.

It was in workshops that I *learned*. True, the method is barbaric and flawed, but it sure does make you learn to write better.

The alchemy goes something like this: You are nineteen years old, or seventy-nine, or forty-three. You write terrible, terrible stories. You know there's something not quite right about them. You know you should revise them, spruce 'em up. But you don't, honestly, know how to do this, sitting alone in your room, listening to classical music, petting your cat. You want to work on your pieces, but you just don't know.

So, you take a workshop. You turn over your precious cat poems, your summer camp story, your little essay about the Pope, to a class of people just about as bad at writing as you are. They tell you your story/poem/essay is really bad. Which it is. You read their work, tell them the same thing. Then, it's your turn again. You try to not muddle things up as badly as you did the last time. Your next story/poem/essay introduces problems you didn't even know were possible to commit, in addition to the regular ones you tried to avoid but couldn't.

But in your second workshop story, you don't send girls off to meet priests on docks to talk about redemption, shrouded in mysterious mist. You make other mistakes, and it's hard and uncomfortable to make them publicly, but you learn.

I think it's because here, in pools of fluorescent light, all over the world, like little secret societies in badly decorated rooms in colleges and community centers, are gathered twelve or so souls truly dedicated to putting words on paper, page after page.

Few people do this.

So many want to. But in the workshop rooms, twelve are gathered, twelve who love words and communication, and the elegance of effort.

It's a weird rite. But it's also beautiful, and kind, and hopeful. People, trying to make words more right. It's very precious, even though you vomit and sob and get worse before you get better.

You get a story ready, you copy it off, and you distribute it. That is a kind of publication that insists, somewhere deep in you, that you are really *writing*.

People read your work in workshops.

Maybe that alone is worth the price of admission.

ON YOUR PAGE: *Exercise 53*

A workshop is only as good as its participants, and the best participants engage and react, rather than quickly judge, criticize, and dismiss. Try this. Take a short story or poem or essay or article from a magazine you are reading right now. Pretend it has been submitted for workshop. What would you say to the author? To the class? Try to come up with a couple of sentences that describe the piece, and what happens in you when you read it. Try to slow down. Try not to say "I liked ..." or "It was good when ..." but rather, "Reading this piece is transporting me to another place and time. When X happened, I really felt Y." Try to give the (not-present) author a sense of what it was like to be the reader, the person on the other end of the equation.

That's the value of workshops, really. You get access to the heads of your readers. It's the one thing you can't know, since you are its creator: What's it like to read my story? Practice "workshop reading." See what happens when you pay attention to how you react and feel when you read. Amazing things will happen to your writing. That's the real workshop secret.

Chapter 29
Ambition

SOMETIMES I FEEL AMBITIOUS.

Sometimes I nap. Often, I nap too much. I am spending the best years of my life napping. I nap *a lot*.

Sometimes I feel if I only practiced what I preach, I could be Joyce Carol Oates, Stephen King, John Updike, writing four books a year.

Often, I fear I will lose my friends if I become any more ambitious.

Ambition. We get afraid of being successful because we are used to things as they are. Change, even good change, is very scary. Would we be us anymore if we took our writing more seriously? No. We wouldn't. It's a little like death. Well, it's exactly like a death. New you writes more. The new you gets good. The old guy, the nonwriter wanna-be, dies.

We all say we want this, to be writers, but I can see why so few folks actually put the time in.

You have to be very fearless to change yourself. It's not very comfortable.

Ambition leads to different friends, different clothes, different habits, a different maybe unrecognizable you. Ambition leads to seeing your parents not as extensions of yourself, but *related* to you—people on the planet with their own hearts and goals.

Ambition is growth.

To be "successful" as a writer you have to imagine clearly and fearlessly what you really want. Do you really want to write a bestseller? Because you could. You could read dozens of them and figure out just how to do it. If you focused on that, it would happen for you. You could read books on successful people and their habits. You could make yourself into that type of person.

But you would have to *not* be the person you are right now.

Most people like who they are right now. They don't want to say adiós to themselves and take their chances on a new self.

Ambition is a constantly wavering rug under your feet. The chasm is exhilarating and scary. What's really "going up the ladder" feels like free-falling down, down into scary space.

A little ambition is a good thing for your writing. Realize that ambition is change, and death. I'm not overdramatizing. It's that hard. Realize that you are going to resist change—the you who is you now doesn't want to die! Of course not! But if you have outgrown this self, you have to say: "I need more. I need a bigger self, one that fits who I am going to be."

You know that real estate wisdom, buy the house you can afford in five years? I'm suggesting you work today with the habits of the writer you are going to be in five years.

Calmly, realistically say what you want for your writing life. Be honest. You can be whatever you want:

A closet writer. (Write every day, never reveal you do so.)

A wanna-be writer. (Talk about what you want to write and how unfair and hard publishing is.)

A nonwriting writer. (Think about your writing a lot. Get complex illnesses instead of words down on paper. Decide you are "busy.")

A duped writer. Say "I'll write later," and know inside you won't. Hang around people who will play this sad dangerous game with you.

A famous writer. (Write every day. Trade work with people a little better than you. Read every day. Go to writing conferences and school. Learn *a lot*.)

A smart, quiet literary writer with a devoted, tiny following.

A one-hit wonder writer.

A struggling-against-himself writer. (Write a couple of times a month. Spend a lot of time listening to the demons who tell you the work sucks. Indulge these voices. Or, drink a lot. The demon voices of No Ambition like that particular weapon especially. Mindless sex, drugs, anything that keeps you from noticing what is good and interesting in your work— do that.)

You *can and are* designing your own career as a writer. What you are thinking about is what you are heading toward.

ON YOUR PAGE: *Exercise 54*

Study writers' lives. Read *The Paris Review* interviews and the *Glimmer Train* interviews and the essays by writers in *The New York Times*. What are the varieties of a writer's life? What are the perks in the career? Who is the boss when a person is a writer? Get more information about what writers do, how they tend their minds.

Read *Publishers Weekly* and other writers' journals. What's the difference between popular and mainstream? What's a genre writer? Who is who? Why? What does a day in the life of a successful writer look like? Most writers will tell you: lots and lots of days, sitting with fear and doubt.

Get a tape recorder and a good friend. You are going to be interviewed. This exercise asks you to let the ambition in you come out. Expect resistance. Proceed anyway. Get into a comfortable place—where you work and write, or eat or anywhere that is "you" in some way. Set the friend up with tea, a snack, and the tape recorder. Give the friend, your interviewer, your list of questions. Again, you have to really do the exercise. You can't do this in your head.

Your questions might include:

> *What kind of writer are you?*
>
> *What are your strengths as a writer?*
>
> *What kind of career would you have as a writer if you could design your own career?*
>
> *What in your childhood led you to want to be a writer?*
>
> *What really leads you to want to write?*
>
> *Describe your typical working schedule.*

Go ahead and steal questions from the interviews you read in part one of this exercise, above. You'll want to be asked about twenty to twenty-five questions. You are asking an inner self, the baby, unformed future fabulous writer within. This is a very powerful exercise.

It will be hard for you to listen to this tape, but you must. In a month or so after the interview, play back the tape, by yourself. Try to listen without cringing (you will cringe). What parts of yourself do you really love here? What parts need more space in your life?

After listening, write for ten minutes. Begin with the words, "Once upon a time ..."

Chapter 30

A Wave Suspended

IF YOU'VE DONE THE EXERCISES IN THIS BOOK, FOUND A WAY to write daily, established a writing community, and worked your way through a few blocks, bad moods, and little loops, you aren't a beginner anymore.

You're on your way.

So what's next?

What's going to be your next goal? Another way of asking this question is, again, why write? What's it for? What's most important to pay attention to as you deepen and grow as a writer?

You have to dig deeper and deeper to find the elements of human nature.

You have to know yourself.

You have to understand yourself better than before. Your job is not to make more money. It is to understand the elements of human nature.

Critic John Lahr writes, "Glamour—the word has its root in the Scottish word for 'grammar'—is an artifice of elegant coherence; it requires distance."

Look at the art and the movies and the television you thrive on, listen closely to the songs that thrill your soul. There's a combination of distance and intensity. That's art. The crafting and presenting of our most profound human emotions so the rest of us have a mirror.

A truly wonderful actress, Dame Judi Dench, compares making art to being underwater: "There's a wonderful abandonment you feel in water. It's very liberating. It's like the unconscious. You're just floating around there and trusting you're going to come up to the surface."

That's the kind of confidence you develop as you move from beginning writing to *being* a writer. You're never totally safe or sure. You're floating. You don't know if your writing is good or not that day, not yet. But you learn to trust that you will come up for air, able to tell later what went on down there.

My best writing sessions feel like long dives underwater. I'm scared I won't come back. But I always do. Living with that ambivalence, learning how to hold my breath, and open my eyes to the dark, weird light—that's good writing.

Critic David Jones says of the actress quoted above, Judi Dench, "Her gift is to step down on the throttle so you don't get the full impact of her passion; you just know there's an enormous amount in reserve. It's like a wave suspended."

A wave suspended.

That's the state you're trying to maintain as you close the pages of this book, and pursue your writing education. Ask, at each turn, does this exercise/book/course/person/program/journal/magazine help me learn to dive underwater?

The longer you can stay in that completely open energetic moment, where everything is just about to come together, and there's nothing you can do about it, that's the moment where learning and growth transform you.

To grow as a writer, you grow as a person. There's no way to work on one without the other.

Successful writers defer judgment. They're kinder to themselves and to other people. They're hungry learners and supportive of other writers. They seek out interesting ways to learn more about writing and art and literature; they go to the party. And contribute to the conversation!

Successful writers look at their resistance to see what it's telling them. They develop a healthy relationship to sitting alone in a room. They give in to bad moods and rely on invitation rather than whips and discipline to get their work done.

Great writers write from their compost, their true material. They offer the reader their very best gifts, not the junky stuff anyone could pick up at the dollar store, but the rare material they've inherited, that they alone can tell.

And, that's you.

You are a wave suspended. You are embarking on a whole new kind of writing life, one that feeds and enriches you and those around you. You will stay the course. You know how to do this, and you know where to find and how to use the tools that will keep you going: journals, classes, books, people.

You can send me an e-mail, or visit my Web site at www.heathersellers.com. I teach classes around the country on how writers focus and concentrate. I want to hear how it's going, and I would love to hear your reactions to the exercises in this book. Some of my students form page-after-page groups and help each other. There's information on the Web site about how to take a year and do the exercises in this book.

You can be a writer.

I hope this book has helped you see, page after page, that you already are.

Go back through this book. Choose an exercise you skipped. If you did them all (good for you!), pick one you hated, one that went horribly. Try it, this time, knowing you can come up for air anytime you want.

As you re-enter this exercise, let yourself get that feeling of "wave suspended"—where you are in the graceful moment doing writing, postponing judgment, about to fly free over the blank page.

Appendix
Recommended Reading

Books on FOCUSING for Writers

Gail Sher, *One Continuous Mistake: Four Noble Truths for Writers.* Drawing from her years of experience as a Buddhist, Sher offers wise instruction on training your mind, quieting down, and focusing. For writers at any level.

Eric Maisel, *Fearless Creating: A Step-by-Step Guide to Starting and Completing Your Inner Work of Art.* This book helped me deepen and intensify my writing practice as no other book has done. Maisel is a generous, wise psychologist who works exclusively with artists. Packed with intriguing exercises to work your creating mind, I recommend this book to every artist I meet. Highly recommended for your writing shelf.

Ursula K. Le Guin, *Steering the Craft: Exercises and Discussions on Story Writing for the Lone Writer or the Mutinous Crew.* This book is essentially a very smart class—for one person or for a group—in writing narrative.

Susan K. Perry, *Writing in Flow: Keys to Enhanced Creativity.* This book analyzes "flow"—that free-form state where most artists say their work truly originates and teaches writers how to deal with blocks, distractions, and fear.

Victoria Nelson, *On Writer's Block: A New Approach to Creativity.* Of all the books on writing and writer's block, this is the best. Nelson understands the varieties, scope, and complexities of writing blocks.

Dorothea Brande, *Becoming a Writer.* A classic and considered required reading in many writing classes. First published in 1934, this volume is simply inspiring. Brande reveals the state of mind you need to be in to write, how to achieve it, and how to keep it.

Linda Trichter Metcalf and Simon Tobin, *Writing the Mind Alive: The Proprioceptive Method for Finding Your Authentic Voice.* This book teaches you how to deepen your attention and release your inner writer, get rid of inhibitions and write emotionally and effectively.

Books on JOURNAL-KEEPING for Writers

Georgia Heard, *Writing Toward Home: Tales and Lessons to Find Your Way.* This is a wonderful book to guide your daily writing practice or stimulate journal entries. I have used it in my classes for years.

Elizabeth Berg, *Escaping Into the Open: The Art of Writing True.* Dozens of exercises, and short, helpful, smart chapters on how to get past your blocks and make fire and passion on the page. Good for beginning writers.

Anton Chekov, *Notebook of Anton Chekov.* When I am stuck in my journal-habit, I like to read these notes and jotted down lines by one of my favorite authors.

Alexandra Johnson, *Leaving a Trace: On Keeping a Journal.* By an award-winning teacher and writer, this guide offers suggestions for journal entries, observation, avoiding writer's block, and turning your journal into a memoir, narrative, or novel.

Sheila Bender, editor. *The Writer's Journal: Forty Contemporary Writers and Their Journals.* Another sneak peek into the minds and hearts of working writers, this book also gives tips on keeping a writing journal.

Going Further With YOUR WRITING

If you are interested in writing stories, poems, screenplays, or essays, there are many guides on how to do so. I have found these the most useful for serious beginners.

Janet Burroway, *Imaginative Writing: The Elements of Craft.* Covers all four genres—fiction, poetry, drama, nonfiction—and is widely considered the best book of its kind.

Donald Maass, *The Career Novelist: A Literary Agent Offers Strategies for Success.* One of the most successful literary agents in New York, Donald Maass has advice for the "big picture" that novelists will need to keep in mind if they are going to write more than one book. A terrific insider's guide to New York publishing, this is required reading for those interested in approaching an agent with a finished manuscript.

Susan Goldsmith Woolridge, *Poemcrazy: Freeing Your Life With Words.* Accessible and thoughtful, this is a good introduction to writing poetry. Lots of interesting exercises.

Jerome Stern, *Making Shapely Fiction.* Jerome Stern's masterful little book holds the secrets to writing fiction. Humorous, sly, and imminently useful. Highly recommended for all fiction writers.

For additional recommended reading selections, visit my Web site at www.heathersellers.com, and see what's on my bookshelf.